GLYNDŴR'S WAY NATIONAL TRAIL

An exploration of
the beautiful heart of Mid Wales

David Perrott

KITTIWAKE

Published by
Kittiwake Books Limited
3 Glantwymyn Village Workshops, Glantwymyn, Machynlleth,
Montgomeryshire SY20 8LY

© Text, map research & photographs: David Perrott 2014
© Maps: Kittiwake 2014.

Care has been taken to be accurate.
However neither the author nor the publisher can accept responsibility
for any errors which may appear, or their consequences. If you are in any
doubt about access, check before you proceed.

Printed by MWL, Pontypool.

ISBN: 978 1 908748 14 0

Contents

	Introduction	5
	Glyndŵr's Way	
1	**Knighton to Llangunllo**	8
2	**Llangunllo to Felindre**	13
3	**Felindre to Llanbadarn Fynydd**	16
4	**Llanbadarn Fynydd to Abbeycwmhir**	19
5	**Abbeycwmhir to Blaentrinant**	22
6	**Blaentrinant to Llanidloes**	25
7	**Llanidloes to Afon Biga**	30
8	**Afon Biga to Aberhosan**	38
9	**Aberhosan to Machynlleth**	45
10	**Machynlleth to Cemmaes Road**	51
11	**Cemmaes Road to Llanbrynmair**	58
	A thinker, but not a farmer	63
12	**Llanbrynmair to Llangadfan**	64
13	**Llangadfan to Llanwddyn**	69
14	**Llanwddyn to Dolanog**	73
15	**Dolanog to Meifod**	78
16	**Meifod to Welshpool**	82
	The Montgomeryshire Canal	89
	Guidance Notes and Useful Information	90
	Distance checklist	92

Machynlleth – about half-way

INTRODUCTION

Glyndŵr's Way carves a very remote and beautiful 135 mile arc which stretches through the hills and mountains of Mid-Wales between Knighton and Welshpool, anchored in the west by Machynlleth. This town was, for a short while in the 15th century, declared the capital of Wales by Owain Glyndŵr, in a place which to many eyes was logically as central a situation for this institution as you can get in the Principality.

From the bleak but beautiful isolation of Beacon Hill Common to the tranquillity of the River Vyrnwy, from the lonely moorland above Dylife to the rolling farmland of the Vale of Meifod, Glyndŵr's Way offers an exhilarating walking experience and exploration of the remote Mid-Wales countryside. The route passes habitats which are nationally important, such as sessile oak woodland with carpets of bluebells, upland mire and heath, ancient hedgerows and un-spoilt river valleys. A particularly notable section is from Penfforddlas to Aberhosan, which bisects part of the Pumlumon massif noted for the extent and quality of its heather moorland, an increasingly rare habitat. Walkers on Glyndŵr's Way will also have the opportunity to observe at first hand the rich variety of wildlife typical of Mid-Wales. Birds such as skylark, buzzard and red kite are commonly seen along the route, and many lanes and hedge banks are rich with wildflowers, particularly in the spring. Mid-Wales also remains a stronghold for the traditional pattern of small fields, whilst some sections pass through or close by common land, wind turbines and forestry, providing an insight into varying types of land management.

But who was Owain Glyndŵr? Perhaps his story has its roots in England's conquest of Wales, which was completed in 1284 under Edward I, when Prince Llywelyn was killed in a skirmish with English forces at Cilmery, near Builth Wells.

Owain ap Gruffydd, Owain Glyndŵr, was born around 1359, the son of Gryffydd Fychan and a descendant of the Royal House of Powys, and of Deheubarth, and also a distant relative of the Tudors. He probably served as an apprentice in law in London, staying at the Inns of Court. He later became Squire to Henry Bolingbroke, King Richard's cousin, and during this period learned his fighting skills, doubtless honed during campaigns in Scotland and Europe. Glyndŵr was one of the very few Welshmen who held estates from the Crown. In 1398, his military career over, he settled on one of his estates near Sycharth in a moated wooden house with great halls and chambers. He married Margaret Hanmer and raised a 'nest of children' amidst orchards, fish ponds, peacocks and fallow deer. But all was not as peaceful as it seemed.

In the late 14th century there was discontent in Wales over punitive taxation and anti-Welsh legislation. The Black Death had left a legacy of poverty, destitution and unrest, and land was being enclosed by unscrupulous owners who wished to pursue profitable sheep farming. Tenant farmers were being dispossessed by rent increases. In September 1399 Glyndŵr's neighbour, Sir Reginald Grey of Ruthin, stole some of his land and, although Glyndŵr tried to regain possession using legal means, the rift between the two men was deepened when Grey insulted Glyndŵr, saying 'What care we for barefoot Welsh dogs'.

Eventually Glyndŵr resorted to force to regain his land, and the spirit of rebellion quickly spread, with numerous attacks against English-owned property. The revolt grew, and soon English towns, and Abbeycwmhir, were attacked by bands of Welsh guerillas. The Covenant Stones, two quartz boulders at Hyddgen, high on Pumlumon, mark the spot were Glyndŵr defeated the Flemings in 1401. On the 16th of September of that year, Owain was proclaimed Prince of Wales, encouraged by Welsh hatred for the English King Henry IV and his Marcher Lords (a noble appointed by the King of England to guard the border). On the 18th of September Owain's motley army rode into Ruthin. By the 24th they had raided other towns and were closing upon Welshpool when they were routed near Shrewsbury. Henry's army arrived the next day, and subsequently subdued the whole uprising. All of the rebels, except Owain, were pardoned.

This peace was, however, short lived and rebellion re-occurred in 1401 when Henry IV passed onerous anti-Welsh legislation. Conwy Castle was burned and Owain raised a second army, and Henry responded, strengthening garrisons and reinforcing castles. A comet which appeared in the sky in 1402 was taken as an omen, since its tail was said to point towards Wales, reinforcing Glyndŵr's reputation as a wizard. His second rebellion grew when he defeated the English at Pilleth, near Knighton, at a place called Bryn Glas. Owain then moved south, and blockaded the castles at Harlech and Caernarfon.

By 1404 Owain had secured Wales and established a Parliament in

Introduction

Machynlleth. In 1406 the Tripartite Indenture was signed. This was a pact between Glyndŵr, the Earl of Northumberland and Mortimer to divide England and Wales between them. He also tried to make an alliance with the French, but this came to nothing, even though he tried a second time, calling a meeting in Machynlleth and sending the famous Pennal Letter to Charles VI, King of France, in March 1406, expressing his wish to have a Welsh Church with bishops appointed from France rather than Canterbury, and to have two universities established, one in north and one in south Wales.

Eventually King Henry became ill, and gave Prince Henry a free hand to campaign in Wales, soon turning Owain into a fugitive. In 1407 the rebellion faded through starvation and a lack of funds, and Aberystwyth and Harlech Castles, both held by Glyndŵr, were under siege. By 1409 they had fallen and in 1410 it was all over. Glyndŵr and his son Maredudd were forced to flee, living as guerillas.

What became of Owain Glyndŵr after 1412 is a matter of speculation. One early 20th century author maintained he died on 20th September 1415 at Monnington-on-Wye. Others believe he ended his days at the home of his daughter Alice and her husband Hugh Scudamore at Monnington Stradell, in the Golden Valley in Herefordshire. But there are also those who hold that he went to live at Pwlliwrch, Darowen, near Machynlleth (a mile or so off Glyndŵr's Way), and others who claim he died near Valle Crucis Abbey in Gwynedd.

Although Owain Glyndŵr's dream of independence ended in the early 15th century, he still remains an icon of Welsh culture, reflected in the increasing confidence of 21st century Wales, now with its own fledgling parliament.

Thanks

This book would never have been completed without the help of Morag, my wife. From giving lifts to and from all sorts of obscure locations at any time of the day, to assisting with the historical research and checking the manuscript, her help has been beyond measure. This fully revised edition was put together with the invaluable help of the current Glyndŵr's Way manager Helen Tatchell, and our grateful thanks are extended to her. We have tried to thoroughly check everything but, if there are any mistakes, they remain mine.

David Perrott

1 • KNIGHTON to LLANGUNLLO
6½ miles

Knighton is known as Tref-y-Clawdd in Welsh, 'the town on the dyke': it was the English who called it 'Knight's Town' during the 17th century, when King Charles had his knights garrisoned in the area, although this name may have been a corruption of 'Cnwc-din', the fort on the hill spur. The town has a colourful borderland history dating back at least to Caractacus, who is thought to have established a fortified settlement between Knighton and Clun to resist the Romans. Later King Offa of Mercia attempted to put a stop to the constant border disputes by reinforcing an existing 6th century dyke in the late 8th century. This substantial earthwork stretches from Treuddyn, north-west of Wrexham, in the north to Chepstow in the south.

William de Braose built a wooden castle in Knighton in the 12th century, on a hill which became known as Bryn-y-Castell, to discourage incursions by the Welsh, and this was followed by a sturdier stone-built structure to the east of Broad Street, and it was around this that the town developed. It was fittingly Owain Glyndŵr who conducted the last major assault on the town in 1402, when he defeated an English army at The Battle of Pilleth (Bryn Glas) and captured Sir Edmund Mortimer. A group of Wellingtonias planted in 1870 on the site of the battle marks the site of a mass grave for the fallen. These events were presaged by the sighting of a comet over Europe in February of the same year, when the bards proclaimed Owain 'the son of prophecy'. Violent thunderstorms were attributed to his supernatural powers. In the midst of such events it is interesting to note that Edmund Mortimer and Owain Glyndŵr soon formed an alliance, which was bonded when Edmund married Glyndŵr's daughter.

Many of the buildings you will see in Knighton date from the 17th century, when it was an important trading and droving centre for east Radnorshire, and its prosperity increased due to its position on the Hereford to Montgomery, and London to Aberystwyth, roads. Indeed in the late 18th century there were five toll gates around the town.

When the railway was built in 1860 it brought a new flush of prosperity as Knighton became a depot for seeds, fertiliser and feed, soon to be followed by tanning, malting and cloth production. St Edward's Church was substantially rebuilt in 1877 on the site of a Norman building, the remains of which survive in the lower part of the tower, which had been mostly demolished in 1756. The timbered belfry is particularly attractive: such structures are common amongst the churches of Herefordshire, and it is this which leads perhaps to the reason

1 • KNIGHTON to LLANGUNLLO

Knighton – where your journey begins

why this Welsh church should have an English dedication, but whether it is to Edward the Confessor, or the Saxon King Edward the Martyr remains a matter of conjecture. If you fancy a pint, or a meal, there is no shortage of pubs and cafés in the town.

The Clock-tower at the junction of the High Street and Broad Street, built in 1872, now marks the start of Glyndŵr's Way and, as you begin your walk, climbing steeply up the hill, you will become increasingly aware of the town's snug position in the valley of the River Teme.

The High Street soon narrows and curves gently up to the Golden Lion in Market Street, where you turn left along Castle Road. Follow this as it bends to the right, giving a fine view down the valley to the left, and ahead. You continue along a narrow lane overlooking the town, eventually going steeply down hill. Cross a road and continue, maintaining your direction down a slightly narrower track. Continue walking beside back gardens and a corrugated iron fence, then pass Weaver's Cottages and carry on along the path. You are now walking beside a stream with trees all around, and the town has, for the moment, disappeared from view.

As a lane joins from the right at Mill Lodge, you fork right up a signed footpath, continuing ahead at the end of a cul-de-sac as signed. Cross the road by Greenacre and walk for a few strides up the driveway towards a house and then turn right just before Woodhouse Close. The narrow path climbs steeply, passing pretty back gardens. At the top of the hill turn right, walk ahead for 30 yards and then fork left in front of some houses. *You can now enjoy a wonderful view over Knighton as you catch your breath.*

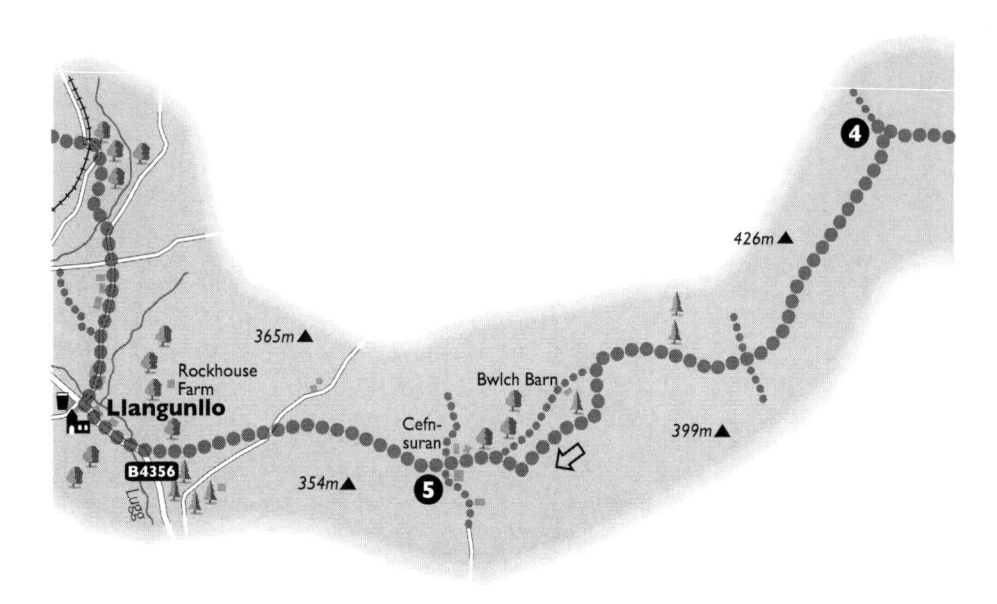

2 Ignore a field gate to your right and continue along the green lane, walking around the northern side of Garth Hill and overlooking the valley. Ignore a stile to your right and continue ahead, and then ignore a path which heads uphill to your left and again continue ahead. Go through a a gate and join a track which comes in from the right and then turn right following the track downhill (ignoring the track which climbs uphill). *You are now walking through a very fine expanse of mixed deciduous woodland.* The path goes through a gate and continues, reaching the next gate, which you also go through. You are still walking through woods, with views over the valley, where Heart of Wales Line trains occasionally rumble by, with a fence to your right. Follow a path down to a house and continue along the main path, which now begins to curve left, leaving the beautiful Teme Valley and continuing around Garth Hill, which rises high to your left. A single track road approaches from the right, and the route of your track joins this, and you continue ahead. When you meet another lane, turn left and follow this lane for a little under half-a-mile. Before you reach the bottom of the hill,

1 • KNIGHTON to LLANGUNLLO

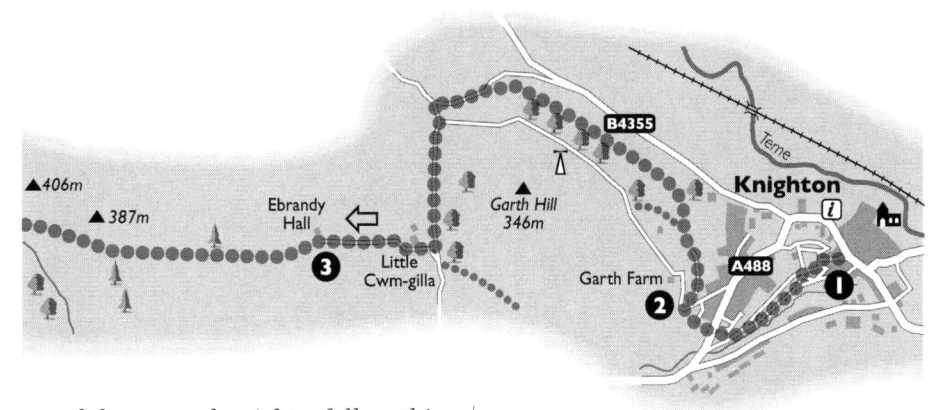

a track leaves to the right – follow this, going slightly uphill and passing Little Cwm-gillia farm. The lane now climbs quite steeply between high banks. *It's a good idea to stop now and again to rest, turning around to enjoy the fine view. You have earned it!*

3 The tarmac is left behind at Ebrandy Hall as you continue walking ahead up the track, still climbing! The track ends at the summit of this unnamed hill at a gate, which you go through. Continue with a fence and a hedgerow to your right. *The view is now a full 360 degrees, and you should stop and savour it.* You then descend the hill, beside a fence and a hedge, with an open view to the left as the track winds ahead up the next gentle hill. The track becomes muddier as you pass through a gate and continue ahead passing a pond on the right, beginning the gentle climb, with the hedge and the fence now to your left.

4 You reach a track and turn sharp left as signposted, to continue ahead when you reach a gate. You then go through a gate, and then three more, and continue with the hedge on your left, and again you start to descend with gentle, green, hills tumbling off into the distance and a clear ridge ahead, then go through a gate. At the field corner continue ahead through a gate with the hedge still to your left. Descend by a small muddy pool and continue, with a fence to your left and lots of bright yellow gorse ahead. A large farmhouse appears. Go through an un-waymarked gate and continue ahead, with a quarry up the hill to your right. Ahead is a gate marked 'No Admittance'. About 10 yards before this gate turn left through a gate signed with a blue waymark indicating 'An Environmentally Sensitive Area'. Walk half-right down hill to a waymark post, where you join a track and veer left to cross a small stream, following the track for a short distance uphill then forking right as signed. Go through a gate, cross a stream and then turn right, to walk with the fence to your right. Go through a small gate in the field corner, join the track ahead, cross a stream and veer left along the track.

11

You pass a fishing pond to your left, cross a cattle grid (or go through a gate), to leave the field and join a track which veers left.

5 Enter the driveway of Cefnsuran. Directly ahead of the entrance to Cefnsuran follow a waymarked path between trees by a tiny stream (don't turn left to walk around the house), which brings you to a gate. Go through and immediately turn left and go through another gate. Walk across the yard and leave it via a waymarked gate along a track. You pass a man-made lake on the right before continuing ahead towards a gate, which you go through. Carry on ahead through trees to the end of the track, then continue ahead to the field corner, where there is a gate. Go through this, then veer right across the field to another gate. Go through to join a lane and turn left. Walk along the lane for 15 yards to a gate on your right. Go through and walk ahead, downhill and through trees. Soon you are following a little hollow pathway which descends into a quiet valley with trees all around. A waymark post appears ahead. Continue with trees on your left to reach a gate ahead, just across a farm track. Go through and continue down the field. Go through a gate in the bottom right-hand corner and continue ahead with a stream on your right. Go through a gate beside a garden and continue down the track beside a house to join a road, where you turn right to reach Llangunllo.

2 • LLANGUNLLO to FELINDRE

9¼ miles

1 In Llangunllo village centre turn right by The Greyhound pub. *This pub was once owned by Bill Matheson, who died aged 92 in 2006 and was thought at the time to be the oldest licensee in Wales. Having stood empty for a while, it is now a welcoming pub with beamed ceilings, and a cosy fire on chilly days. Unusually, the lovingly restored bar is round the back (like The Dovey Hotel at Cemmaes Road). Accommodation is available in a separate, very comfortable, cottage (01547 330003).* Go straight across the crossroads at the top and then, when the road curves to the right, go straight ahead through a gate and follow the path downhill to a little metal footbridge, and cross it. Now continue uphill, veering right and with a fence to your left. Go through a gate, walk up to a road and turn right. Walk under the railway bridge and continue straight ahead along the track, crossing over a cattle grid (don't turn right along the road).

2 Pass Nayadd Fach and go through a gate to continue uphill along the track, going through a second gate. Leave the track and turn left through a gate (well before reaching the barns ahead). Turn right to follow the field boundary to a gate. Go through and shortly turn left to veer half-right to the top corner of the field, where you go through a gate to walk with fence on your right. Go through a gate and continue with a fence to the right. Go through another gate and follow a wide green track with a fence on either side. Eventually the track descends to join a farm road. Continue ahead, beginning to climb. *Stop now and again to catch your breath and look back to enjoy the view of the mountain ridges stepping away to the horizon. It is very typical of Mid-Wales, with very few trees.*

As you progress the track becomes wide and clear, crossing open moorland and you are, for the first time on Glyndŵr's Way, conscious of your elevated position. You steadily slog uphill until you pass between conifer plantations to reach a gate at the junction of several paths. Ignore the path to your right to go ahead for a few strides, then turn left to cross Beacon Hill Common. *This is Crown Estate land covering an area of 4667 acres and administered by the Radnorshire Wildlife Trust.*

3 Walk with conifers on your left and cross Short Ditch, an ancient earthwork, and continue. Soon you must veer to the right on the track as waymarked, ignoring a gate to the left. Stay on the track, which skirts around Pool Hill – *and gives lovely views along a valley to the right.* Eventually the clear track ends, and you continue ahead along a green track as signed, surrounded by a wild expanse of

13

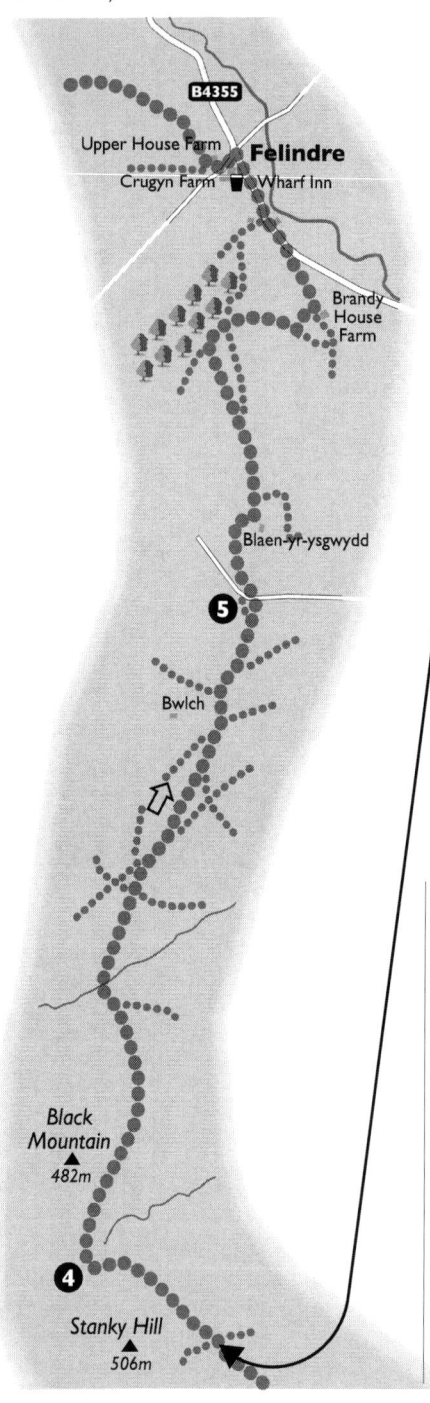

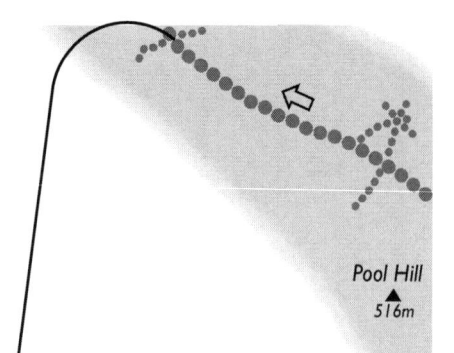

undulating heather upland with domed summits each side. The track meanders relentlessly on, gently rising and falling and offering the occasional tantalising glimpse of a side valley. As you approach Stankey Hill the track is again green and pleasant underfoot, and as you near its shoulder, a cwm comes into view ahead. Look out for the waymark post here which directs you to turn sharply right along a less distinct, but still well-defined, track across the low ridge of the Black Mountain.

4 The track continues over the moorland to an isolated waymark post on the horizon, where moorhens avidly defend their nests during the breeding season. Follow the faint track as it descends, eventually reaching a rough and muddy section to cross a bridge over a little stream and continue to the right, now gently climbing with just sheep and the calls of moorland birds for company. The gentle climb uphill continues along a wide jumble of tracks, which soon condense into one clear route, with a waymark post to reassure you. Views open to the left and ahead is a clearly

2 • Llangunllo to Felindre

defined track snaking uphill, the last climb on this section before Felindre. At a track junction continue ahead to go through a gate and a stile and carry on ahead over Beacon Hill, soon climbing a stony track which veers right. A lonely waymark post appears.

by a waymark. In the bottom corner of a rough and unkempt field you reach a gate. Go through this and carry on with a fence to the left. Go through a gateway and continue with the fence still on your left. *There are good views here over Felindre, and a spectacular view over the valley ahead, bisected by the River Teme, where the hills are divided by small fields and punctuated by the odd farm house.* Go through a gate and continue down the track, zig-zagging steeply towards Brandy House Farm. Go through a gate beside the farm, then turn left to go down to the road. At the road, you turn left to reach Felindre.

5 The track then meets a road, which you cross and then veer half-left to a fence corner. Veer right, keeping the fence to your right. When you reach a gateway go through it and follow the track to the right. Very shortly you reach a second gate on the right. At this point you veer off to the left by a waymark post, to head towards a second post, enjoying the very fine wide views across valley to the right. Carry on along a faint track as directed

3 • FELINDRE to LLANBADARN FYNYDD
7½ miles

The Wharf Inn (01547 510373), is on your left, in Felindre. This traditional pub, with a cosy bar, is open *from 20.00 'til late (not Tues)*. It serves real ale and bar snacks, and has a log burner to enjoy when the weather is cool. You continue past buildings in Felindre to reach a crossroads, where you turn left by a large wooden shed/barn. Walk along the lane for about 80 yards and then turn right through a gate to walk across a yard. Go through gates, pass the farmhouse and turn right to leave the yard through another gate. Follow the clear track uphill to a gate, ignoring a gateway to your right, off the track. Continue ahead along a green track incised in the field on the apex of the hill-slope – *with expansive views all around*. Go through a gate and continue uphill, with just a few straggly trees to your right. The old hedgerow comes and goes as you continue to climb, finally passing a plantation of conifers. *Gradually the fine view to the north here will become inaccessible as they grow*. Go through a gate as you approach the Great Wood, which is just over the fence to your right. Having left the wood behind the track becomes more clearly defined, and soon you pass through a gate and continue downhill along an enclosed section of track, which bends to the right and approaches Rhuvid.

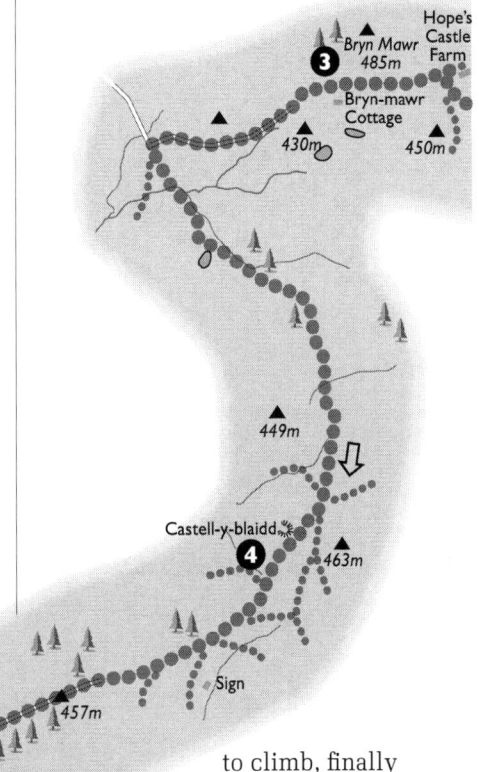

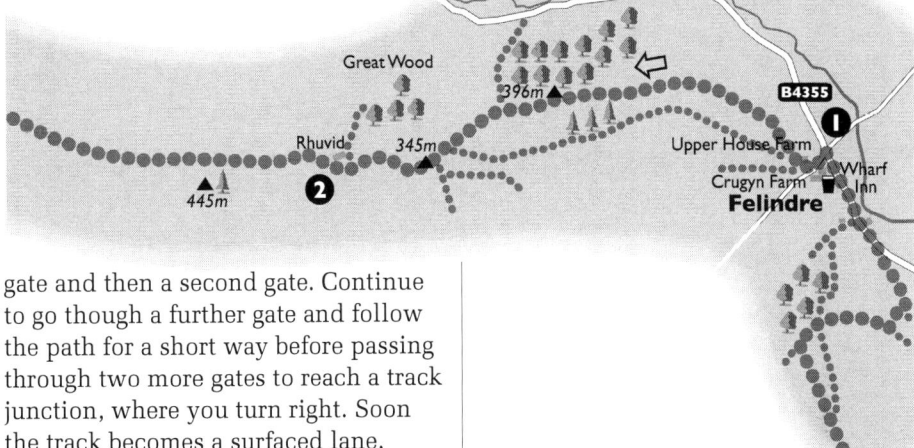

3 • Felindre to Llanbadarn Fynydd

2 Pass by the house using two gates and immediately begin climbing a stony track. Go through a gate and continue, passing a small conifer plantation on the left. Go through a gate and then a second gate. Continue to go though a further gate and follow the path for a short way before passing through two more gates to reach a track junction, where you turn right. Soon the track becomes a surfaced lane, and you turn left to follow this, going through a gate and continuing along it. *In the valley to the left a stream has been dammed to form three ponds, and there are more ponds beside Brynmawr cottage.*

3 Continue along the road and, just before a steep dip, turn left over a cattle grid and carry on along a clear track. When this track bends to the right, go straight ahead through a gate, immediately crossing a bridge over a stream and continuing ahead over a field to reach a gate. Go through and follow the track uphill and to the right. You pass a tree-edged pond on your right and carry on climbing, with a valley to your left, to a gate. Go through this and continue uphill, veering left to a gate. Go through and enter an old plantation. Follow the track and soon leave the wood through a gate to veer right over the brow of the hill ahead, heading for a small bridge. Carry on ahead to a gate, which you go through, veering slightly right to follow the track which stretches over the right-hand side of the hill ahead, passing another waymark post. Cross a farm track and carry on uphill. When a fence appears on your left, fork right off the main track onto a green track, by a waymark post. *On the summit of the hill to your right is Castell-y-blaidd (castle of the wolf). There is a wonderful view from the summit, but unfortunately no right-of-way to give you official access. This is the site of an unfinished 13th century castle, which was probably abandoned for the better situation of Tinboeth, about four miles to the south-west.*

4 Go through a gate and walk to a waymark post ahead, passing a marshy patch. Veer right to a gate by a livestock pen. Go through to join

17

On the way to Abbeycwmhir

the road and turn right. Go through a gate and continue, enjoying the fine view ahead. *Soon you'll notice the tall turbines of a wind farm on the horizon to your right.* Pass a few straggly trees at Fron Top before descending to Llanbadarn Fynydd. A short way beyond the new farm house at Esgairwyndwn look out for a stile to the left. Cross this and continue downhill, with a hedge on your right, then veer away left to go through a gateway. Now walk to the right, parallel to a fence. Ignore the cattle grid on your right and continue down to a stile. Cross this and carry on down to Llanbadarn Fynydd, where you turn left. Pass a memorial stone to reach the New Inn – *which serves real ale and meals, has a nice garden and welcomes children.*

4 • LLANBADARN FYNYDD to ABBEYCWMHIR

8¼ miles

1 Walk along the pavement at Llanbadarn Fynydd passing the shop and café, with the New Inn to your left. Carefully cross the road, and maintain your direction, now beside the Afon Ieithon, a trout stream. Pass a church below you to the right and then turn right to follow a road which bends again to the right. Cross the bridge and continue, passing some houses and then following a hairpin bend to the left. About 25 yards after the bend, turn right, but not sharp right, along a track.

You now start gently climbing. Go through a gate ahead and carry on with a fence on your left, passing through a gateway and continuing to a stile beside a gate, before trees.

2 Go through and turn left, to walk with a fence on your left. Go through a gate and walk ahead, over a wide field, veering left and looking for a waymark post amongst the gorse. When you have located it, follow the direction indicated. The marshy hollows of this route guide you through a wide boggy patch, where there are boardwalks to help keep your feet dry. All of this is eventually left behind as the track becomes clearer. Now you are walking along the side of a gloriously lonely valley and, when you have almost given up hope, a waymark post appears, to reassure you. *As the track descends, the views widen, with glimpses of the Brecon Beacons and the Black Mountains on the far horizon. You pass a plantation on your left, which is framed by a lovely overgrown stone wall. Cross a track, which enters forestry land, and carry on ahead by a bank, keeping the fence to your left. Be sure to ignore a track which forks away uphill to your right. Walking beside another fine rough stone wall on the left you suddenly notice the noise of traffic emanating from the valley road below, a sound unheard for many miles.*

Continue your descent, following a sunken path and with conifers to the left. After zigging and zagging a fence joins from the left and eventually you reach a wooden gate beside a house. Go through and continue downhill. Go through a gate and continue. Go through a gate and carry on, following the track as it bends right through a wooden gate into Tynypant farmyard. Turn left to pass through a gateway onto the road. *On a near summit to the north-east, just across the Afon Ieithon, is Tinboeth, which may have been Roger Mortimer's Castle dating from 1282, and known as 'Dynbaud'. It stood until 1322, when it was surrendered to the King following the conquest of Wales. It then fell into ruin and now little remains to be seen, apart from traces of the gatehouse.*

19

Glyndŵr's Way

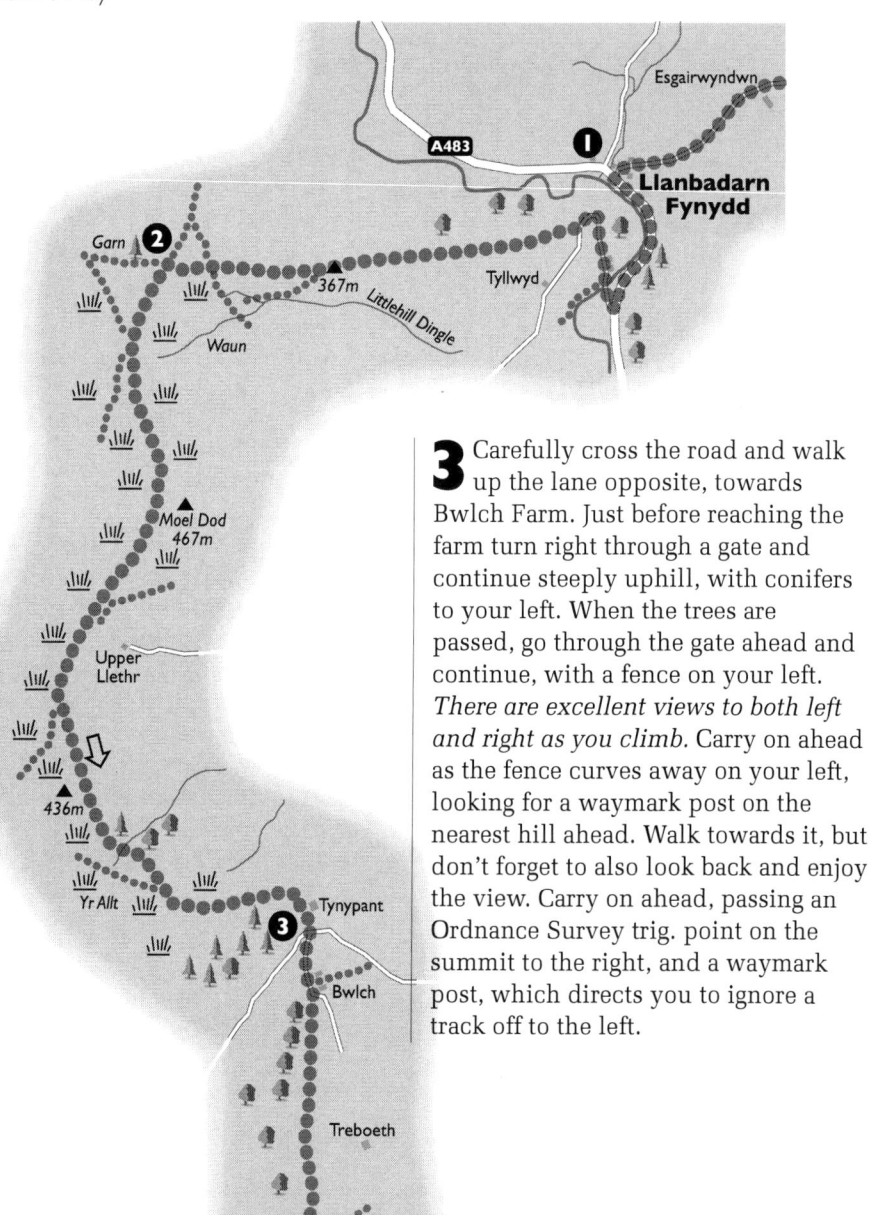

3 Carefully cross the road and walk up the lane opposite, towards Bwlch Farm. Just before reaching the farm turn right through a gate and continue steeply uphill, with conifers to your left. When the trees are passed, go through the gate ahead and continue, with a fence on your left. *There are excellent views to both left and right as you climb.* Carry on ahead as the fence curves away on your left, looking for a waymark post on the nearest hill ahead. Walk towards it, but don't forget to also look back and enjoy the view. Carry on ahead, passing an Ordnance Survey trig. point on the summit to the right, and a waymark post, which directs you to ignore a track off to the left.

4 • Llanbadarn Fynydd to Abbeycwmhir

4 When the path descends to a dip between summits, turn sharp right at a waymark post and follow the route down off the mountain. Note the dark conifer plantation ahead – your path descends and then goes right through it. So, turn left at the waymark post, walking down the cwm to go through a gate on the right, and enter the trees. Follow the very pleasant path downhill, which winds its way through fine mixed woodland, and later conifers. It is, however, quite muddy in places. Leave the forest through a wire and metal gate and go down to another gate. Go through and continue downhill and to the right. Cross a concrete bridge and carry on ahead over a cattle grid, to soon rise up to a gate to reach a road. Turn left and walk along the lane, eventually passing an old wooden bridge in a dip to your left.

5 Climb steps up to a stile up on a bank to your right and continue as waymarked, soon descending to the left. Cross a stile on the path through woodland, which ends with a handrail beside a slope to a stile at the bottom. Cross this stile, then turn right to cross a footbridge and continue up the slope to a gate. Go through this and carry on, keeping the fence to your right. Go through a gate on the right to walk behind Brynmoil, keeping the fence to your left. Descend to a gate, go through and carry on along a track. This soon becomes a road, and you maintain your direction as you join the main road to reach Abbeycwmhir. Pass the ruined abbey on your left to reach the church and the Happy Union Pub. *This traditional village local has been run by the same family since 1937, and has no TV, jukebox or fruit machines. It also functions as the village shop and post office, and has two self catering holiday cottages available. Sandwiches and soup can be provided by prior arrangement (01597 851203). Look out for the fascinating old sign fixed to its side wall.*

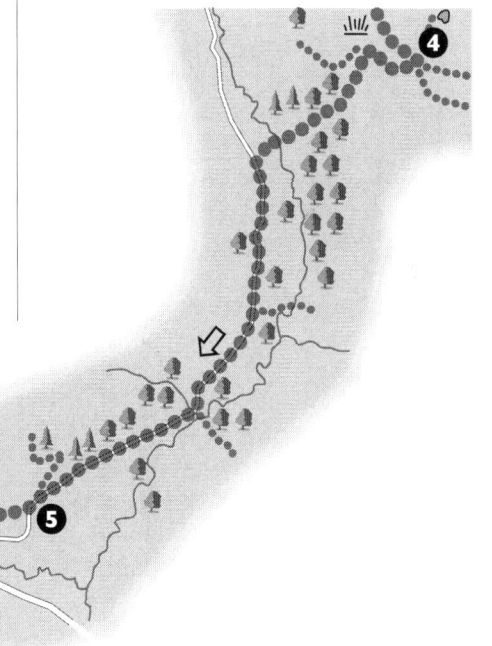

Glyndŵr's Way

5 • ABBEYCWMHIR to BLAENTRINANT
6¾ miles

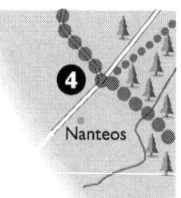

1 From the church in Abbeycwmhir walk to the right, with the Happy Union pub to your left, and turn right by the old petrol pump. As you walk up the lane the church is soon below you to the right, with water tumbling from an arch on the edge of the graveyard. When you reach a gate, go through it and continue along a green track. You start gently climbing with a stream below you on the right, and forestry woodland ahead. When you reach a wooden gate, go through it and continue along a sunken green lane, which continues to gently climb. When you reach a waymark post at a track junction continue ahead. At a forest road cross straight over and carry on ahead – the track now dips, and you stay on this, ignoring the forest road. When another forest track crosses obliquely, continue ahead and downhill. Another forest road makes an oblique crossing, and once again you continue ahead and downhill as waymarked. There is now a small stream to your left and, beyond that, a road. When the path dips, continue ahead for about 20 yards and then turn left to cross a footbridge. Continue along the track, which in wet weather has a small stream running along it, and soon it becomes a hollow lane brightened with bluebells in the Spring. It then climbs to join a lane, where you turn right.

2 Walk along the lane past Fishpond Farm. At a waymark post on the left, turn left and continue through farm gates heading towards Lower Esgair. You are now walking on tarmac, and climbing very gently. Go through a metal gate by a house and veer right along the track, leaving the house behind. Stay on the track as it bends to the left, ignoring a little stile and a gate to your right. You continue gently climbing and pass a double-fenced hedge on your left and continue on up the hill.

When you reach a gate, go through it and then veer off the track to the right to go through the next gate immediately ahead, and continue with the hedge to your left. Go through another gate and carry on, keeping slightly left with the hedge on your left. *While you are gently traversing the brow of the hill the views to both right and left are excellent.* Go through a gate in the field corner and turn right, continuing uphill along a farm track towards a gate. Go through this gate and veer half-right uphill towards a gate which is just below the near horizon. Don't go through, but turn left, to walk with the fence on your right. You are still climbing, so if you need to catch your breath, *stop and enjoy the splendid view over the valley, with bare hills to the left and large areas of forest to the right, enlivened with a sprinkling of farmhouses.* Go

22

5 • Abbeycwmhir to Blaentrinant

to your left and the very rounded hill summit to your right. The faint profile of the path can be seen as a notch in the hillside ahead, by the fence. When the fence leaves your path, heading off half-left, you continue ahead towards a waymark post. *The view on the northern side has now opened up – it is a wide valley with a few scattered trees, framed by distant low hills.* You pass a fenced conifer plantation to the right to reach a track by a fence ahead.

3 Here you turn right and at last start walking downhill towards Bwlch-y-sarnau. At the bottom of the hill you reach a gate. Go through this and continue ahead, passing a small bungalow. Soon you join a road and turn left, ignoring the fork in the road to your right. Pass the church, the graveyard and the community centre to your right, to turn right down a track by a red telephone kiosk. Go through two wooden gates to the right of the house and carry on through the next gate and turn right, keeping the fence to your right, to walk up to a gate. Go through this and carry on, with the fence still to your right. *Again you are walking up to the brow of a hill, with superb views all around.* Go through the first metal gate on your right into a small enclosure and walk across this to a gateway on the opposite side. Go though and carry on, keeping a fence

Glyndŵr's Way

ahead beside a sunken track, with a fence to your left. Go through the small wooden gate ahead and continue, still with the fence to your left. The field is very rough, so just pick your own route down to cross a small bridge and reach another small wooden gate ahead. Go through this and follow the path ahead through a large expanse of young trees. The waymark posts leads you through until a final waymark post appears and eventually you reach a forest road, which you join and turn right.

You carry on to eventually cross a concrete bridge over a stream. Continue along the main track to reach a wooden gate through which you leave the forest to join a road.

4 Turn left. After 20 yards turn right along a minor road, and stay on the road as it turns sharply right, and then left, passing cottages at Waun. *It is a wide open landscape here, in a broad valley enclosed by rounded mountains and speckled with forest plantations under an open sky, all very peaceful and quite remote.* The road continues through this panorama and eventually starts to gently climb. As you reach the hill-summit the road turns sharply left – but you fork off right along a forest road and continue climbing surrounded by trees. There are fine views to the north-west, with a wind farm on the horizon. When a track joins from the left you continue ahead. As the plantation ends you reach a metal gate – go through and continue along the clear track to reach Trinnant, and a road which connects with the B4518.

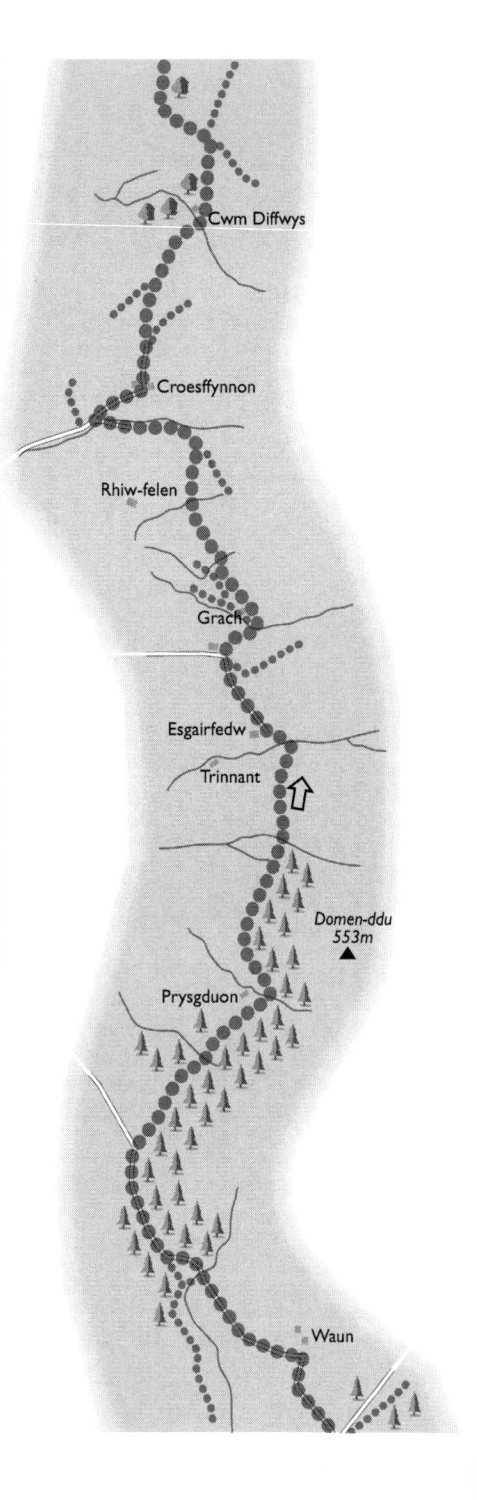

24

6 • BLAENTRINANT to LLANIDLOES
8½ miles

1 By the entrance to Trinnant farm you come to a wooden gate. Go through this and continue ahead (do not go down the lane to the house). The track becomes a road at Esgairfedw and you continue, walking slightly uphill and going through a gate beside a cattle grid. Stay on the road when a track leaves to the right. When the road bends to the left and starts to descend, and a track joins from the right from behind trees, you continue straight ahead as directed by the fingerpost. Turn right (but not very sharp right) through a gate by a cattle grid into the farmyard at Grach and carry on, passing barns to the left. You continue through a set of gates, descending to a stream and crossing a footbridge just below a little waterfall and reaching a stile beside a gate. Cross this. Continue ahead along a clear track to reach a gate, which you go through. Carry on ahead along a path over pasture. Cross a very small stream and go up to a gate, walking above Rhiw-felin and soon with the tumbled remains of an old wall on your left. You join a track by a waymark post and turn left. Go down hill and through a gate, and continue along the track. The surface becomes tarmac when a track joins from the left. Continue and, when you join another road, turn very sharply right by the fine sign for Cloesffynnon, painted on an old mangle.

2 Go through the gate by the house and continue along the road, climbing steadily. As you near the summit of this hill take the track off to the left, walk ahead for 20 yards and then turn right. Follow the track over a cattle grid beside a gate and continue walking beneath the wind farm, which is up to your right. *The views are now becoming a little more dramatic, the hills are a little more pronounced, and the horizon promises some challenging summits.* Go though a gate by buildings and continue along the track, passing through another gate and veering left with the track, and then right down to a ford, which you cross and continue, going through a gate and climbing the track, passing Ffrwd Fawr, which has been tastefully restored. The path continues climbing up to gate, which you go through, and then veer left down to a second gate, which you also go through, to follow the track, initially steeply down hill and then less so. Go through a gate and follow the track, which bends to the right. *The hillside to your left is covered with a fine variety of deciduous trees, with the windfarm dominating the tops to your right.* You now start to descend amidst a very pretty landscape, and soon the sound of tumbling water emanates from the cwm on the right. You zig-zag down to the valley bottom and approach a stream.

25

The entrance to Croesffynnon

3 Do not cross this stream but turn sharp left to walk along the track, with the water to your right. The track fords the stream, but walkers can use the footbridge thoughtfully provided, and then carry on. Ignore the first gate on your right and continue uphill as the track become rougher. Soon a waymark post directs you to cross a stile to your right. Now walk half-left up the field to reach a stile before woods. *The approach is very steep, so stop now and again to catch your breath and enjoy the view.* Cross the stile and turn left, following the track and going through a gate. The track continues its steady climb amongst deciduous trees. The severity of the climb is mitigated by a splendid view to the left – *clear hilltops above forest, with the odd isolated farm.* Eventually you reach a road and turn right, to continue climbing. *The full expanse of the windfarm is now visible on the summits to your right.* Eventually the road peters out as you approach a cattle grid. Cross this, ignore the fork on your right to Penybanc and continue ahead and slightly uphill. Eventually you cross the summit of the hill. *An absolutely splendid view opens ahead over the valley of the River Severn.*

Go through a gate and continue ahead, ignoring a gate to your right, but keeping the fence to your right.

6 • Blaentrinant to Llanidloes

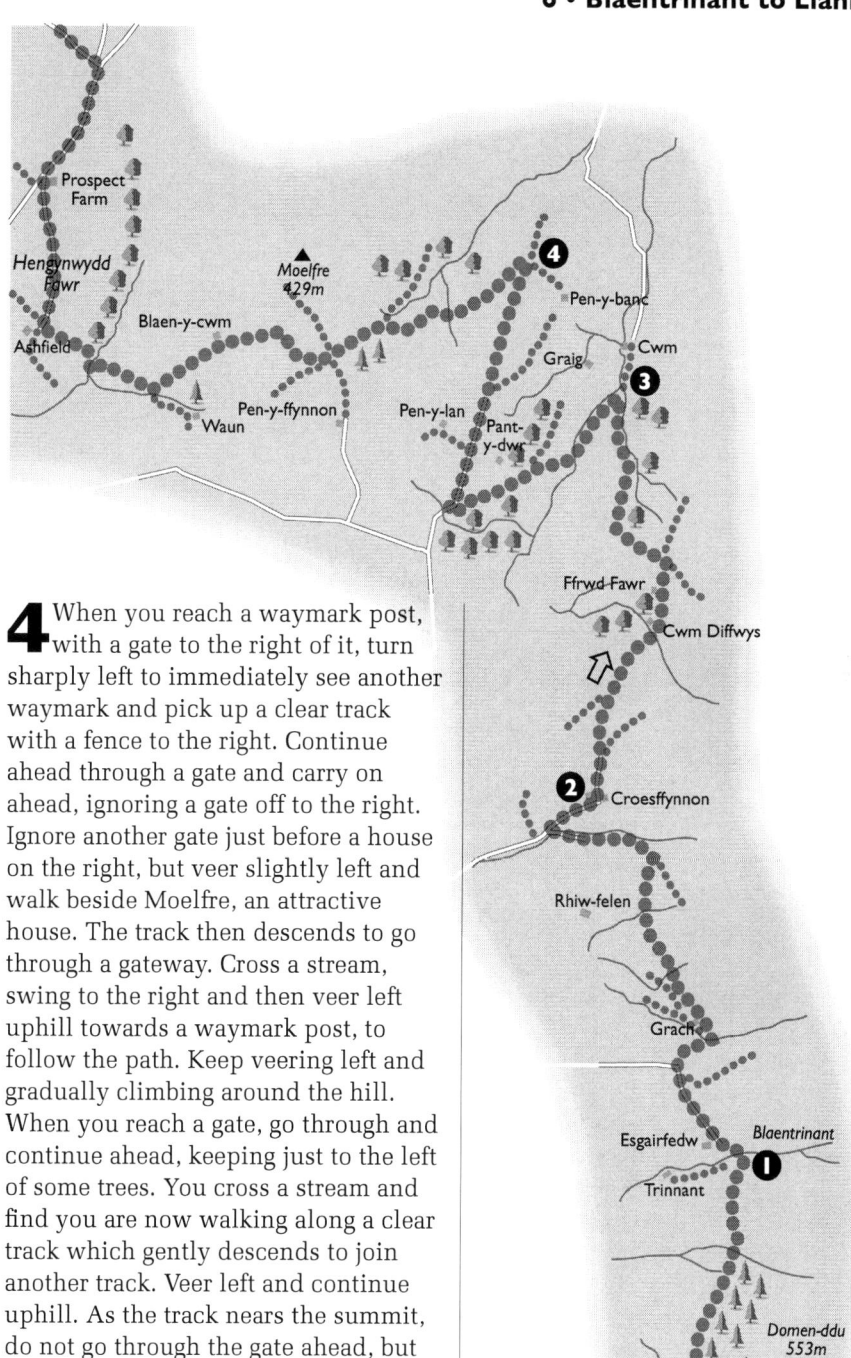

4 When you reach a waymark post, with a gate to the right of it, turn sharply left to immediately see another waymark and pick up a clear track with a fence to the right. Continue ahead through a gate and carry on ahead, ignoring a gate off to the right. Ignore another gate just before a house on the right, but veer slightly left and walk beside Moelfre, an attractive house. The track then descends to go through a gateway. Cross a stream, swing to the right and then veer left uphill towards a waymark post, to follow the path. Keep veering left and gradually climbing around the hill. When you reach a gate, go through and continue ahead, keeping just to the left of some trees. You cross a stream and find you are now walking along a clear track which gently descends to join another track. Veer left and continue uphill. As the track nears the summit, do not go through the gate ahead, but go off the track to the right, cross a stile

Glyndŵr's Way

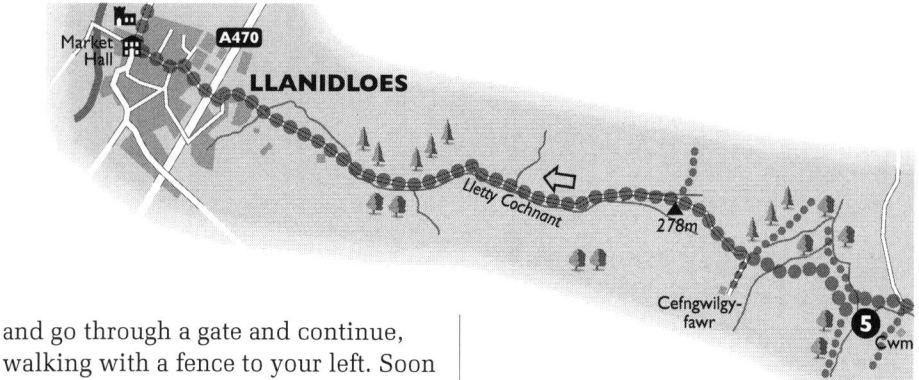

and go through a gate and continue, walking with a fence to your left. Soon you reach a gate on your left, where a green track crosses your route. Look for a waymark post and walk ahead and just slightly to the right as indicated. You cross rough pasture and, as you reach the brow of the hill, you will see a gate ahead of you.

Go through and turn sharp right to walk with a fence on your right. Go through another gate and continue ahead to a second gate, which you also go through and then turn sharply left to walk to a gate. Go through and walk half-right across the field. As you cross the brow you will see a waymark post ahead. When you reach it turn right and walk to a track, where you turn left downhill. Ignore the track which leaves to your left over a cattle grid and go through the gate ahead and walk with a ditch and a fence on your left. Go through a gate and continue ahead with the fence to your left. As you reach the bottom of the field look for a waymark post tucked in behind a tree. Turn right here and walk with the old banked hedge to your right. Go through a gate. You then descend quite steeply as a fence joins from the right. *You are now walking above a lovely tree-lined cwm.*

5 You descend to a stream, cross the bridge and stiles and turn right, to follow the path uphill in a wooded glade. Keep climbing steeply, ignoring little paths which branch off to the right and then, after climbing a steep slope, you arrive at a waymark post and gate. Continue ahead, climbing the field with the hedge and the fence on your right. Continue through a gate and then go through another gate to join a road, where you turn right to walk along the road. When you reach a T junction, turn right and continue. You descend to a road junction, with a magnificent view ahead. Turn left. *You then pass the pretty Chapel Baptist Church to the right: this was founded in 1740, rebuilt in 1850, restored in 1905, destroyed by fire in 1954 and finally (we hope!) rebuilt in 1957.*

The lane passes a red-brick house on the left and then bends to the right, where you veer off left and walk down a very wet field, with a hedge to your left, to reach a stile, which you cross and then turn right. You then turn sharp left at a waymark post to zig-zag downhill towards the stream. Look

28

6 • Blaentrinant to Llanidloes

The Market Hall, Llanidloes

for a stile on your right and cross it, and then immediately cross the bridge and stile. Don't turn sharp right as you come off the bridge, but walk uphill and follow the path half-right as directed by the waymark post. As you climb you join another path: just keep swinging to the left as you continue uphill. The path then curves around to the right and carries on climbing. When a hedge joins from the left continue straight on along a clear path, ignoring a gate to your left. When the path splits, ignore the green path to your left and continue ahead, crossing a tiny stream and bending to the right uphill to a gateway.

Go through the gateway and continue up the field to a stile. Cross it and continue walking ahead along the road. Although the approach to Llanidloes is by road, it is quite quiet and pleasant – *progressing down a valley with a stream on your left, with an occasional block of conifers to break up the grassland beneath the surrounding low peaks. The views ahead are good.* The lane continues its descent and gradually the first signs of Llanidloes appear. You pass a mini roundabout and shortly after this the road curves to the left – here you turn right between houses to join a path which crosses the by-pass via a footbridge. You pass the handsome old railway station building standing to the right. *This dates from 1864 and was, in turn, the head office of the Manchester & Milford Railway, the Cambrian Railways and the Great Western Railway until the line finally closed in 1962.* You then pass the fire station and continue ahead along Cambrian Place, which joins Great Oak Street, passing the imposing Town Hall on the right. *This was built in Classic Renaissance style as a gift to the Borough by the Davies family of Plasdinam in 1908.* Walk ahead to the handsome Market Hall – *the only surviving example of a half-timbered market hall in Wales.*

29

7 • LLANIDLOES to AFON BIGA

9 miles

From The Market Hall walk along Long Bridge Street, passing several pubs and St Idloes' Church, tucked away behind buildings on the left, along Picton Street. This church is a very handsome, squat and sturdy building, with a massively-built 14th century stone tower topped by a 'Montgomeryshire' belfry. Be sure to go inside to see the five arches of the rebuilt 13th century arcade, which was taken from Abbeycwmhir around 1542, standing beneath a very fine hammer-beam roof, decorated with shields and carved angels. Continuing along Long Bridge Street you pass a useful Spar grocery on the right before reaching a small roundabout. Here you turn left to cross the bridge, with Somerfield Park, a handsome Georgian House, overlooking Severn Porte, the confluence of the rivers Severn and Clywedog. Now take the first turning on the left, to walk along Westgate Street, passing a pretty Victorian Terrace as the road begins to climb. Pass Tan yr Allt, the last cul de sac to your right and, just beyond this, turn right to walk along a path above bungalows to your right, with rhododendrons to your left. The path climbs steadily, giving a pleasant view over Llanidloes. You are now entering Allt Goch, which is common land. You must, of course, keep to the right-of-way across here, since the popular belief that common land is generally open to the public is incorrect. *The woodlands are now owned and managed by Llanidloes Town Council, and were acquired in 1936 from the Morris-Eyton family. Trees here include oak, sycamore, beech, birch, rowan, holly, hazel, Scots pine and Douglas fir.* The path continues climbing, and waymarks indicate that you are now sharing your route with The Severn Way – *the longest riverside walk in Britain, stretching fully 210 miles from source to sea.* Carry on ahead when a track joins from the left, and eventually the route levels out and you continue ahead, enjoying the willow-tunnel sculptures beside the path. Ignore a path which leaves to the right and continue ahead along the track for about 100 yards, then fork left, up through the woods as directed by a waymark post. Take care to maintain your direction, as this path could well be overgrown during late summer, and look out for the waymark posts which beckon you ahead, climbing all the while. Go through a gap and carry on ahead, looking out for the next waymark post to guide you, which signals a slight change of direction to the left as you begin to descend. Look for a further waymark post, where you turn left to walk with a fence to your right. Just before corrugated-iron farm buildings on your right a waymark post confirms you are still travelling in the correct direction. You emerge from

7 • Llanidloes to Afon Biga

The remains of Bryntail Mine

the trees and scrubland onto the edge of a golf course and, before you reach the St Idloes Golf Club clubhouse, you turn right through a gap in the fence as waymarked to cross a cattlegrid and walk along a tarmac road.

2 When a lane joins from the left, before a black-and-white timbered house, turn left. You pass farm sheds on the left and a farmhouse on the right and continue ahead through a gate, ignoring a lane and another gateway to the left and another gate into the field to the right. By the first gate on the left, turn left to pass through and walk with the hedge to your left. *At last views of the uplands to the north-west become apparent.* Cross a stile and continue ahead, with a fine view over Fan. Cross a stile and veer half-right to descend a field to reach a gate in the corner, which you go through to join a road and turn right. Follow the road for a short way as it bends to the left downhill, and then turn off left along a track as the road leaves to the right. Don't enter the garden, but take a stile over to the right. Now walk down to a stile, keeping the fence to your left. Cross this stile and continue ahead with the hedge still to your left and Van directly ahead. Pass through a gate in the hedge and continue, crossing the brow and dropping steeply downhill to a stile. Cross this and continue, still with the hedge to your left, to walk down to a gate which you go through.

31

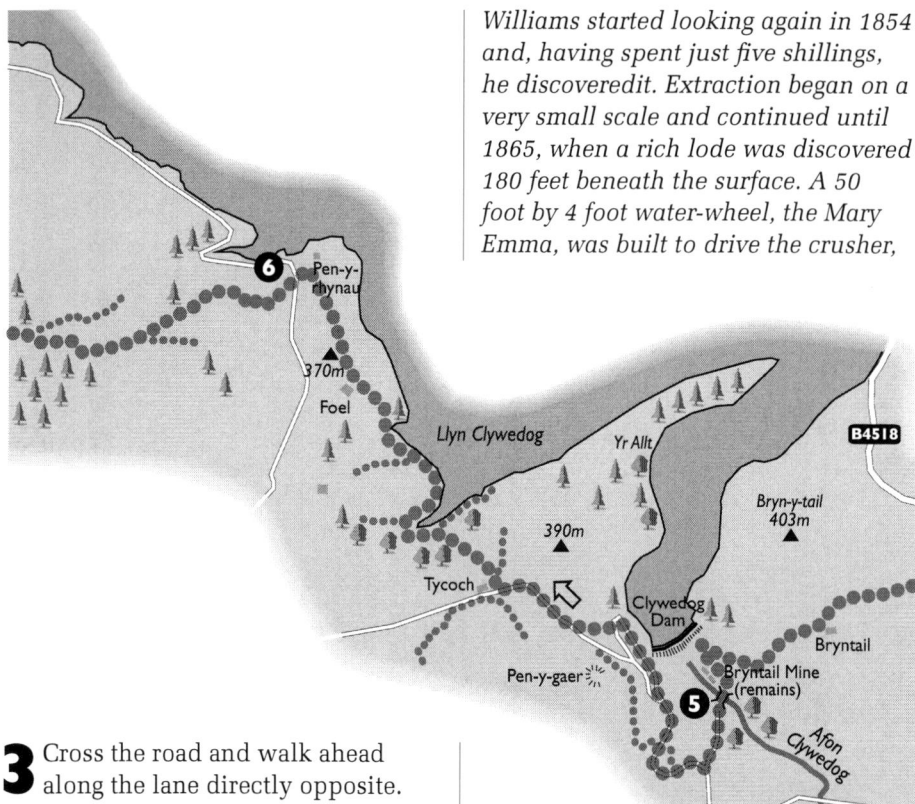

Williams started looking again in 1854 and, having spent just five shillings, he discoveredit. Extraction began on a very small scale and continued until 1865, when a rich lode was discovered 180 feet beneath the surface. A 50 foot by 4 foot water-wheel, the Mary Emma, was built to drive the crusher,

3 Cross the road and walk ahead along the lane directly opposite. Shortly after the road bends to the left, look for a waymark post by a large tree on the right, and walk as directed uphill across rough ground, rich with bluebells in the Spring, to reach a gate: go through and then continue along a track, with a hedge to your right. Pass a stand of mature Scots pines and continue along the track as it bends to the left.

Below you to the right are the disused workings of Van mine, and soon the Van pool appears. *Van mine was once the most productive lead mine in Britain which, in its heyday, brought great prosperity to Llanidloes. The search for the lode began in 1850, and was initially unsuccessful. Captain*

and in 1868 the mine was sold for £46,000. Soon an experienced observer commented that the mine contained 'one of the finest and richest lodes I ever saw', and shares began to rapidly increase in value, with the mine soon being worth over £1 million. Its prosperity was such that a branch of the main line railway was laid from Caersws, initially carrying freight and later passengers. In 1870 the mine yielded an unprecedented 4370 tons of ore, almost twice as much as its great rival Dylife, which is passed later on Glyndŵr's Way. By 1876 over 700 men were employed, and a 70 inch

7 • Llanidloes to Afon Biga

Cornish pumping engine was installed. Further unexpected discoveries of ore prolonged the life of the mine, but closure finally came in 1921, by which time its total output had totalled 96,739 tons of lead ore and 28,424 tons of blende (the common ore of zinc). Cross a stile beside a gate and follow the track uphill towards a waymark post beyond the old mine workings, which are still visible on the hillside. As the clear track you are following bends left to pass to the left of the summit of the hill, you carry on straight ahead along a fainter green track. Pass the summit of Garth Hill to your left and continue ahead to a gate. Go through and follow a fenced and tree-lined green lane. Go through the gate at the end of this fenced section and turn left to walk down a small field, with a drainage ditch and the remnants of a hedgerow to your right, towards a waymark post. Crossing a marshy patch you reach a fence, where you turn right to walk across very rough pasture, with the fence and another drainage ditch to your left. When you reach the field corner, cross a bridge over the ditch and carry on ahead, with the fence still to your left. Go through a small gate and continue ahead, gently climbing with the fence and the hedge still to your left. Pen y banc farm is over to your right. Just before you reach a wide metal gate in the field corner, turn sharp left to go through a gate, then turn sharp right to walk with the fence, and a lane, to your right.

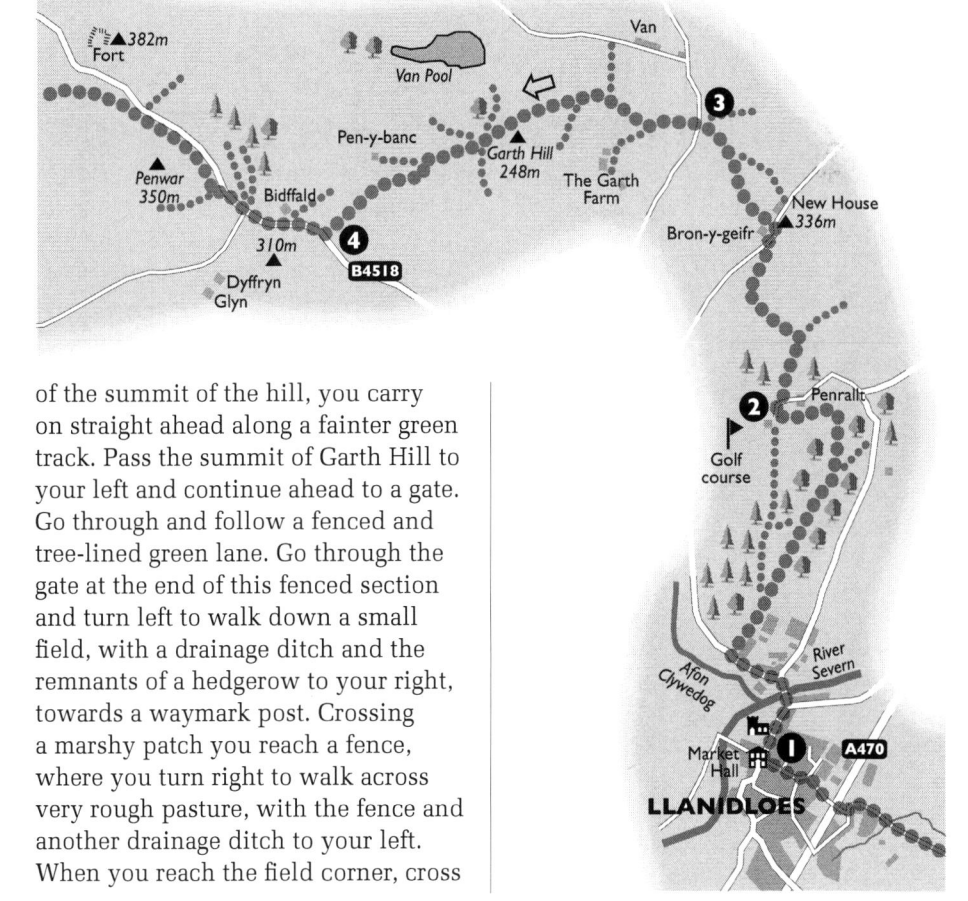

33

Clywedog Dam

4 Go through the gate ahead, walk up to the road and turn right, watching out for traffic. Fortunately there is a green verge where you can take refuge as necessary. Pass the road-sign to Llyn Clywedog and the lead mine and carry on along the road for about 100 yards to a fingerpost on the right, where you turn left off the road up a short track to a gate. Go through this and turn right to walk parallel to the road. Descend to a gate, go through and turn left to walk along the farm road. *(Several thousand tons of lead ore was extracted from shallow workings around here in the 1930s by Isaac Jones).* On a straight section of this farm road, and before it veers left, look for a fingerpost on the right. Veer off the road as directed by this, across the grass to a gate. Go through this and walk half-right, slightly uphill, to a bridlegate. Go through and continue along the top of the field to the next gate, and go through. Cross a farm track and go through the gate opposite. Walk slightly downhill across the enclosure and, when a path appears, follow this down to a waymark post which directs you to turn right to a gate. Go through this to continue along the clear track, passing more old buildings and abandoned mine-workings to your left. Go through a gate and soon the track begins its descent into the valley. *Abandoned mine workings become more prominent.* As the dam comes into view continue on down the track, which curves to the right. Go through a small gate and continue. The track swings down the hill towards the dam, overlooked by the rather boxy and functional control-room on the far side. As you zig-zag down the valley side, the remains of the Bryntail mine buildings appear below you and to

7 • Llanidloes to Afon Biga

the right. When you have finished the descent, go through a gate and down steps to walk past the now very tidy remains of the old lead mine. *The Bryntail Mine is a very ancient enterprise which exploits the eastern end of the Van lode. It is recorded as being worked in 1708, but then fell into disuse until a revival during the early 1800s, when a 25 x 5 foot water-wheel was installed, having been transported by a coaster from Cornwall to Aberystwyth. The mine's most productive year was 1851, when 384 tons of lead ore were extracted, but from then on losses gradually accumulated, in spite of changes of ownership and management. A very fine 60 foot diameter water-wheel was installed in 1870, using a 6-inch rope to pump one of the shafts. The company acquired an adjacent mine in 1870, and new shafts were sunk, but all to no avail. The New Van Consols & Glyn Company formed in 1882, and further shafts were sunk until the whole venture collapsed in 1884.*

5 Cross the wooden footbridge over waterfalls and turn sharp right, keeping the Afon Clywedog to your right. Now follow the track as it bends left uphill and away from the dam. When you reach a road veer right uphill, with houses to your left. At the top of the hill turn right, to walk along a road, initially following the sign which directs you to the Lakeside Drive and Picnic Site. As you approach the summit of this steep hill the road forks: take the right fork. Pass very handsome toilets and a balcony on your left, with splendid views over the dam and the lead mine to your right. *Clywedog Dam is a round-headed mass concrete buttress dam, and was the tallest in the British Isles at the time. It regulates the flow of water in the River Severn and is 235 ft tall and 752 ft long, with a maximum depth of water of 212 ft. A massive 11,000-million gallons of water is impounded, covering 615 acres and being 6 miles long. Work began on 6 April 1964 and ended on the 22 December 1966.* As the road beside the reservoir makes a sharp hairpin turn to the left, you go through a gate on your right and begin climbing, with the remains of an old wall to your right. Head towards the waymark post on the horizon ahead and, when you reach it, veer slightly right towards a signpost, with the road just to your left. When you reach the road, turn right, cross a cattle grid and continue.

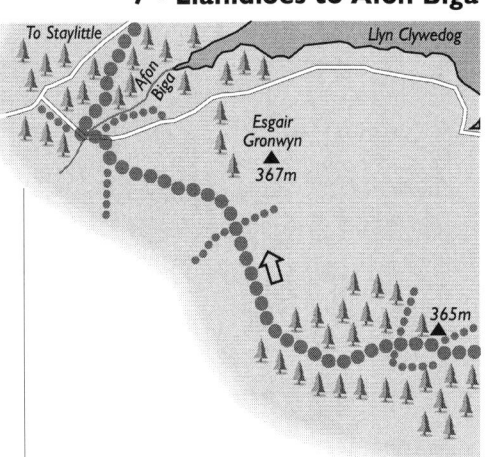

The road bends to the left and starts to descend. You pass a pretty and ornate hedge and turn right as signed. Go through a little wooden gate beside a larger gate, then turn left to walk by the house to reach a stile, which you cross. *There is a very fine view of Llyn Clywedog ahead.*

Continue with a fence and a hedge to your left. Go through a small wooden gate and walk down a fenced path. Go through another wooden gate and descend steps towards the reservoir. Turn left above the water, to continue walking with the water to your right. Cross a little inlet stream on two bridges and continue along a narrow undulating path above the water. Cross a footbridge at the head of an inlet, walk ahead for about 20 yards and then turn right to walk along a narrow path with the water still to your right. *The sound of halyards (a rope used to raise or lower the sails) slapping against masts (in season) announces that you are approaching the Clywedog Yacht Club.*

Climb up through a small stand of trees and proceed ahead through a kissing-gate. Take the road ahead and to the left (not down to the water's edge) to pass the sailing club. *Each summer weekend there is plenty of activity here, with an assortment of craft: yachts, dinghies and sailboards, plus a lively café where the sailors gather to discuss their exploits.* Cross a cattle grid and then, about 50 yards up the hill, veer off the road to the right to reach a gate. Go through this and turn left to walk with the fence to your left and Clywedog to your right. Cross a small stream on a boardwalk and continue, crossing another boardwalk. Now, having crossed the end of a little inlet, you veer away from the water, walking uphill and tending to the left through trees, following a faint path up to a gate.

Go through this and look for a waymark post below Foel. Continue ahead as directed, below the ruins of Foel, and then walk diagonally uphill, with Clywedog to your right, to reach a gate in the field corner. Go through this and continue along a not very distinct path ahead. Continue uphill as directed by the next post as Clywedog again comes into view, and soon you are walking downhill. Carry on ahead at the next post and, as you cross the brow of the hill heading towards a road beside the reservoir, a waymark post directs you to turn left and walk down to the road.

6 Maintain your direction along the road, to walk through a kissing-gate beside a cattle grid. Now cross the road to walk through the gate opposite and continue ahead, following a green track across a field. Pass through a gate, ford a stream and follow the track as it bends right and then left and climbs the hill. The track then swings through an old gateway and continues.

The track contours around the hill and enters a dip, with a row of trees ahead – head for the gap in the trees, where you will reach a waymarked gate. Go through this and continue ahead, initially maintaining your altitude. You will see a waymark post ahead in a gap in another line of trees: pass this and, still maintaining your height and direction, walk to the next post, where the path starts to descend. You soon pick your way down to the stream, which you cross on a wooden bridge and then walk up to a gate to enter the remains of a forest.

Follow a clear track through this

7 • Llanidloes to Afon Biga

Clywedog Yacht Club

felled area of trees, with a stream initially down to your left. The track eventually bends sharply right and climbs up to a gate. Go through this and turn left, to walk with a fence to your left. When the fence heads away sharply to the left, turn right to walk the short distance across the field and up to a gate. Go through this, turn left and immediately go through a second gate and continue along the track.

When the forest track begins to swing around to the left, fork right along a clear, waymarked, forest track. Leave the plantation through a gate and walk slightly right, crossing rough pasture with a fence over to your left. There are patches of very wet and boggy peat to negotiate as you walk down the field. Gradually veer away from the fence to reach a gate, not far from a small conifer plantation. Go through the gate and follow a rough track downhill, veering to the left. *You are now in the midst of a quite bleak and open landscape consisting of rough grazing and marsh, with just conifer plantations to break up the panorama. The only farm in sight is Nant-y-Gwrdu.* Go through a gate and continue along the track, but do not go through the next gate. Instead, veer off to the left along the path downhill. Head for a gate at the corner of the farm's enclosure, but when you reach it do not go through. Instead walk down the side of the enclosure with the fence to your right and a stream to your left. When you reach a track entering the enclosure turn left and cross the stream via the culvert and follow the track around to the right. Cross a ford to reach a gate to the right of a road bridge. There is a pleasant picnic site here, beside the Afon Biga.

37

8 • AFON BIGA to ABERHOSAN
9¼ miles

1 Cross the Afon Biga and continue along the road, crossing a cattle grid and then turning right along a forest road. Veer a little to the left and walk initially with the trees to your left and following the waymark posts. Soon the track rises and enters the trees as you carry on ahead. A little footbridge takes you over a stream as you continue, walking up a green track, surrounded by undergrowth which is quite sumptuous and mossy, and interspersed with bilberry bushes. At the top of the track you join a road and turn right. *The view ahead is quite pleasant, with some tempting higher distant peaks beyond.* You then cross a cattle grid and leave Hafren Forest on a route shared with National Cycle Route 8, passing a weather station to the right and continuing along the road, crossing the bridge over the Afon Lwyd. Follow the road as it swings right and climbs and, at the top of the hill and just before the road swings gently away to the right, turn off left along a track. Go through a gate and continue along a very rough road to reach a gate. Go through this and veer off slightly to the left of the track which leads to a farmhouse, walking over rough ground to reach a footbridge. Cross this and walk up to a gate, which you go through and carry on ahead. Join a track and veer left to follow it as it swings around to the right to reach a gate (ignoring the track which branches off to the left). Go through the gate and continue along the track, passing a small quarry to your left. *The landscape is now becoming that of open moorland, broken with dense forest plantations.*

A fence joins from the right – as you walk to the corner post of the fence, turn half-right when you reach it, proceeding down to a gateway below. Go through the gate and turn left, to walk with the hedge on your left. Cross a bridge with two gates on it and continue ahead, with the fence now away to your left. The gate you are now heading towards can be reached by following the line of electricity poles. Go through the gate, cross a track and continue ahead.

2 Pass through two more gates in front of Llwyn y Gog farm and walk along the track overlooking a broad and green valley. When you reach two gates, go through them and then veer left to walk with the fence to your left. Pass through a gate and continue ahead towards a kissing gate. Go through this and walk down steps to a lane. Go through a gate, cross a bridge, go through a second gate and continue. When the road bends right, go towards Felin-newydd. You continue ahead, climbing a steep slope to a gate. Go through, cross the track, go through the gate opposite and walk up a hollow lane. Continue

8 • Afon Biga to Aberhosan

Leaving Llyn Clywedog

climbing up this hollow way to reach a waymark post, then continue to a second post where you turn left to go through a gate and turn half-right. Walk up to a second gate, go through it and continue ahead up the field to a waymark post. When you reach the post continue ahead to a gate. Cross this and veer to the left to walk with a fence on your right. *As you approach Dylife you cross a high undulating plateau with excellent views of the surrounding mountains, although your immediate surroundings are just tussocky grass conspicuously inhabited by sheep, but enlivened with bird-song, and the almost unbroken song of skylarks, during the spring.*

Go through the next gate and carry on, now with the fence on your left. The track you are walking along is quite ancient; the exposed rock has been worn down by the passage of innumerable cart wheels. You round a corner and the few remaining houses of Dylife come into view as you soon pass a post at a track junction.

3 *Turn right here if you wish to leave Glyndŵr's Way to descend the hill, and perhaps visit the Star Inn, where you can enjoy real ale and a meal. It seems certain that mining took place at Dylife during Roman times, with a substantial revival occurring at the start of the 18th century. The Company of Mine Adventurers reported shafts at 'Delivia' in 1691, although the mine suffered from flooding, but it was not until 150 years later, with the discovery of the Llechwedd Ddu lode, that the mine enjoyed its most*

39

productive period. In 1851 300 men, women and children were employed here, when the largest water-wheel ever erected in Wales, the Martha Wheel, was used for pumping and drawing. Its diameter was 63 feet. When the mine was taken over by a new company it was equipped with the most up-to-date machinery in the country, with the shafts equipped with colliery-style winding cages. The Boundary Shaft was pumped using a 60-inch Cornish steam engine, with drawing being achieved using a 50-foot water-wheel situated over a mile away. How the problems of friction, weather and signalling were overcome on this installation still remains a mystery. The mine's best year was 1863, when 2571 tons of lead ore was raised, a record second only to Van mine (see the previous section). The village of Dylife at this time had a post office, a school, several pubs and, of course, several chapels. Within ten years, however, the mine's output rapidly declined and its owners, wisely trading on past success, managed to sell it for £73,000, a vast sum at the time. The decline continued in spite of new works, and the Dylife enterprise finally ceased operations in 1884.

Continue ahead through a gate, and carry straight on. You are following a green track which crosses undulating high moorland – *with views of Dylife down to the right, a fine valley ahead and to the right, while behind is the vast wind farm on Trannon moor, above Carno.* You continue climbing towards the Roman fortlet, on a track which is almost certainly very ancient, with the undulating summits of the Pumlumon range to the left. You go through a gate and continue along a green track. Soon you pass an elaborate TV aerial to the right, while to your left are the low embankments which once carried the walls of the fortlet at Penycrocbren, a remote outpost of the Roman Empire.

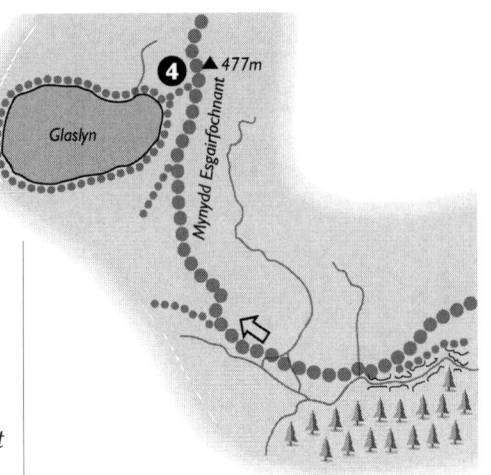

Penycrocbren translates as 'Gallows Hill', and was the scene of a grisly discovery in the 1930s, when a skull in cage was unearthed. It was the head of the mine blacksmith, who over two centuries ago had killed his wife and daughter and thrown their bodies down a mineshaft. His crime was discovered and he was tried, found guilty and then forced to make his own gibbet cages, before being executed. The corpse was then left on display, as a warning to others. The skull and the gibbet are now displayed in the Welsh Folk Museum at St Fagan's, Cardiff.

Continue ahead, now descending very gently with some of the mining remains of Dylife visible to the right. Go through a gate and continue ahead

8 • Afon Biga to Aberhosan

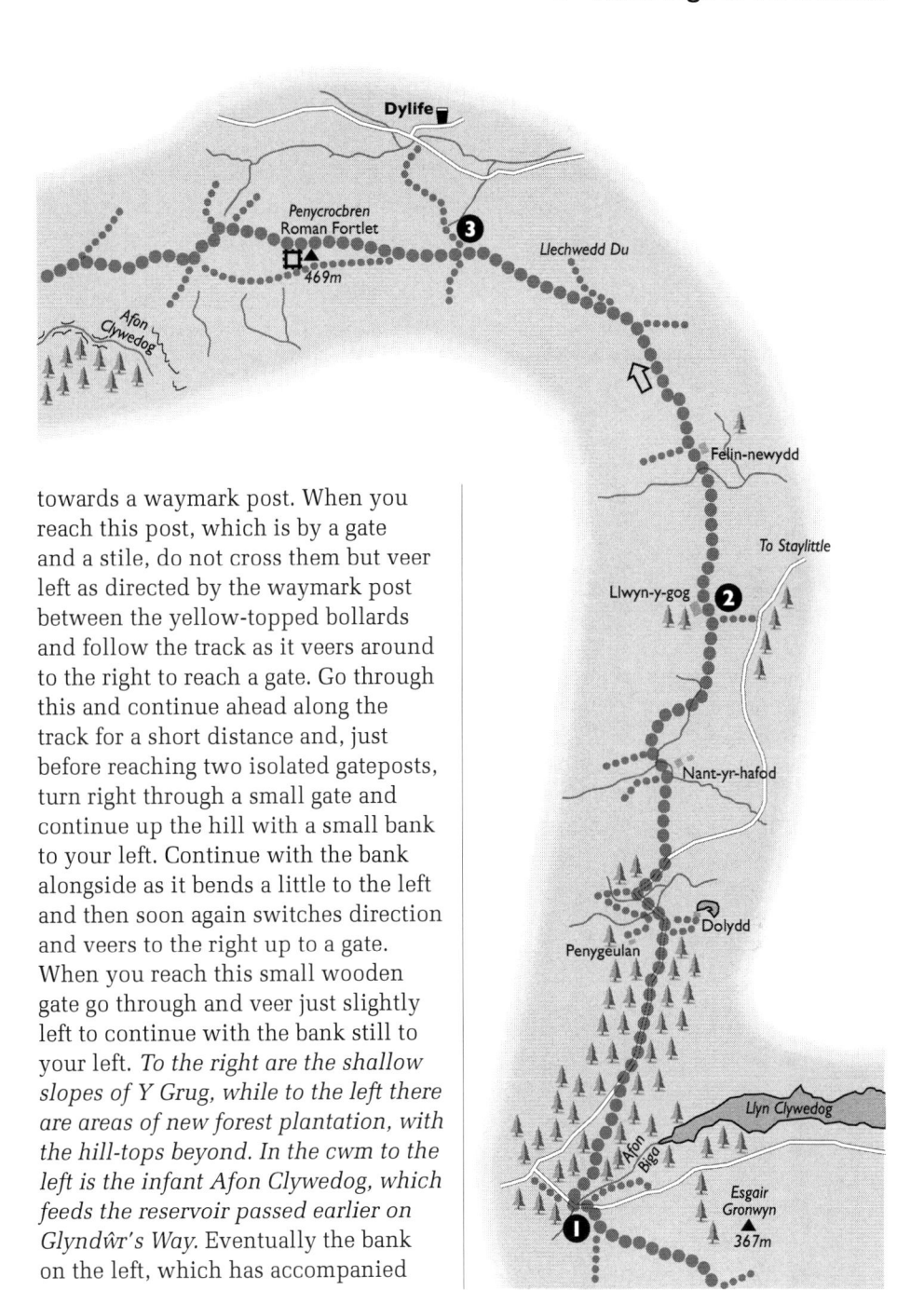

towards a waymark post. When you reach this post, which is by a gate and a stile, do not cross them but veer left as directed by the waymark post between the yellow-topped bollards and follow the track as it veers around to the right to reach a gate. Go through this and continue ahead along the track for a short distance and, just before reaching two isolated gateposts, turn right through a small gate and continue up the hill with a small bank to your left. Continue with the bank alongside as it bends a little to the left and then soon again switches direction and veers to the right up to a gate. When you reach this small wooden gate go through and veer just slightly left to continue with the bank still to your left. *To the right are the shallow slopes of Y Grug, while to the left there are areas of new forest plantation, with the hill-tops beyond. In the cwm to the left is the infant Afon Clywedog, which feeds the reservoir passed earlier on Glyndŵr's Way.* Eventually the bank on the left, which has accompanied walk as directed. Cross a stile and follow the track, until a waymark post appears. When you reach the post, fork left and pass the spoil heaps and faint remains of the Cyfarthfa mine. *This was an unsuccessful venture which began around 1842 and ended – having produced only 100 tons of lead and copper ore – with a lawsuit in the Court of Chancery around 1878, when water the mine was using was considered to be to the detriment of*

the route for the last mile or so, bends down into the cwm, but you continue ahead along the clear path. Go through a gate and continue ahead along the path. Another minor path eventually joins from the left by a waymark post – here you can make a short diversion along this to catch a glimpse of the waterfalls, and then return to this point.

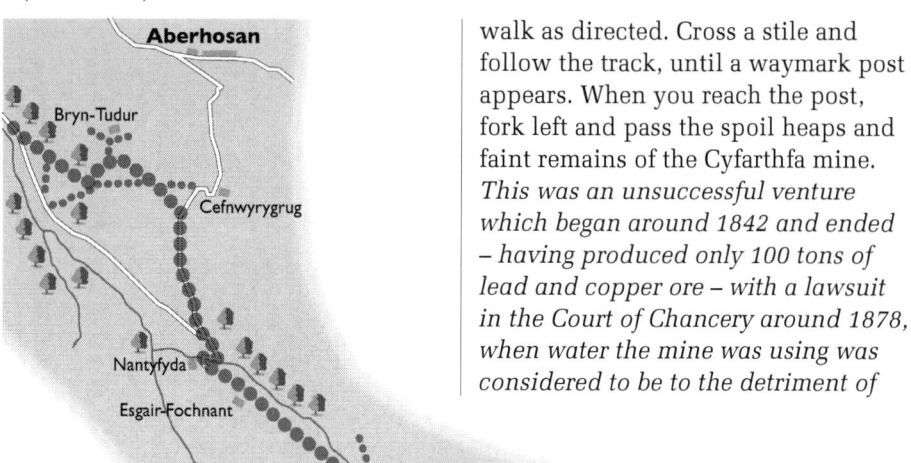

Continue ahead and start a steep zig-zag descent (be careful in wet weather, it can be slippery) to a bridge, which you cross to then go through a gate. Continue uphill along the path with waterfalls and a wood to your left. Again, take care if the ground is wet (*although wet weather does make the falls more spectacular!*). At the top of the short climb veer to the right to reach a waymark post. Now

fulling mills near Machynlleth. As you continue along the track you can see, over to the left, the broken dam of the lake, itself fed by a long leat and a 'cut

8 • Afon Biga to Aberhosan

Glaslyn

and cover' tunnel from Glaslyn, which once fed water to the mine machinery. Carry on to reach a waymark post, where you rejoin the track and turn left. Continue, and look out for the waymark post which directs you to leave the main track and veer to the right, to follow a green path to reach a waymark post, where you again veer right following a fainter green path. You then negotiate a wet patch before reaching the next waymark post, where you continue ahead as directed. The distinct path disappears, but you maintain your direction over the bog, heather, couch grass and bilberries to eventually reach a fence, where you turn right along a stony track. You then follow a track beside a fence, with Glaslyn away to the left. *The mountain directly ahead of you is Foel Fadian, the highest point in Montgomeryshire at 1850 feet. There is a fine walk around Glaslyn and, in spite of its appearance, this diversion through the nature reserve would take you less than an hour to walk.*

4 Cross a cattle grid by the entrance to the reserve and continue ahead and, as the track swings gently to the right, the view down the cwm of Nant Fadian begins to open. *Although nothing can be seen, you are close to what must have been one of the most remote and inaccessible mines in the district, worked in the 1870s by Captain Edward Williams of Dylife. It is reported that the Moel Fadian mine produced just 25 tons of copper ore.* Now look out for the waymark post on your left, which directs you to turn left along a track. You follow the track over a low summit as it bends to the left and begins to descend beside the cwm. A spectacular view confronts you and, on a very clear day, you can see Cardigan Bay.

On the way to Machynlleth

The path now begins to descend very steeply down the track. *The view ahead now is quite stunning.* When you reach a waymark post, stay on the main track, which turns to the left and continues downhill. Continue along the track, still descending downhill and zig-zagging to a gate. Go through the gate and carry on along what is now a green track. Pass through a gate and continue along a superb example of a green track above a steep valley lined with woodland, and still with a wonderful view of mountains ahead. *Down in the valley, almost hidden from view, is the pretty cottage of Cwm-hafod-march, a single storey building originally used as a shepherd's summer residence.* Go through a gate and continue ahead – *after the wildness around Dylife, it is extremely pleasant to walk along this charming, verdant valley.*

You pass a small caravan park to the left to go through a gate and walk by the house of Esgair-Fochnant. Continue along the track, which descends and makes a hairpin turn by Nantyfyda. Continue along the road, ignoring a gate to the left, and continue as it swings left uphill. When the road forks, go to the right, walking steeply uphill. *Red kites can often be seen here, wheeling around effortlessly on thermals as they lazily stalk their prey.* The tiny village of Aberhosan lies a short distance ahead along the road, beyond Cefnwyrygrug farm.

9 • ABERHOSAN to MACHYNLLETH
9½ miles

When the road south-west of Cefnwyrygrug ('the ridge of the heather men' – referring to Glyndŵr's men) swings to the right, you turn off left through a gate as waymarked, and follow the track. Pass through a gate and continue ahead, following the track as it bends left and then swings right, passing a waymark post. Go through a gate to enter a rougher tree-lined section and continue downhill to a road, where you turn right. You are now walking along one side of a steep valley, with trees all around and the pleasant gurgling sounds of a stream, which feeds the Afon Hengwm, below and to the left. When you join a road which approaches from the left, continue ahead, passing a telephone box. About 50 yards further on, at the next road junction, turn left to cross a bridge, then continue ahead up the hill. The roads bends at first to the left, and then to the right, as it continues climbing.

On Bryn Glas Common

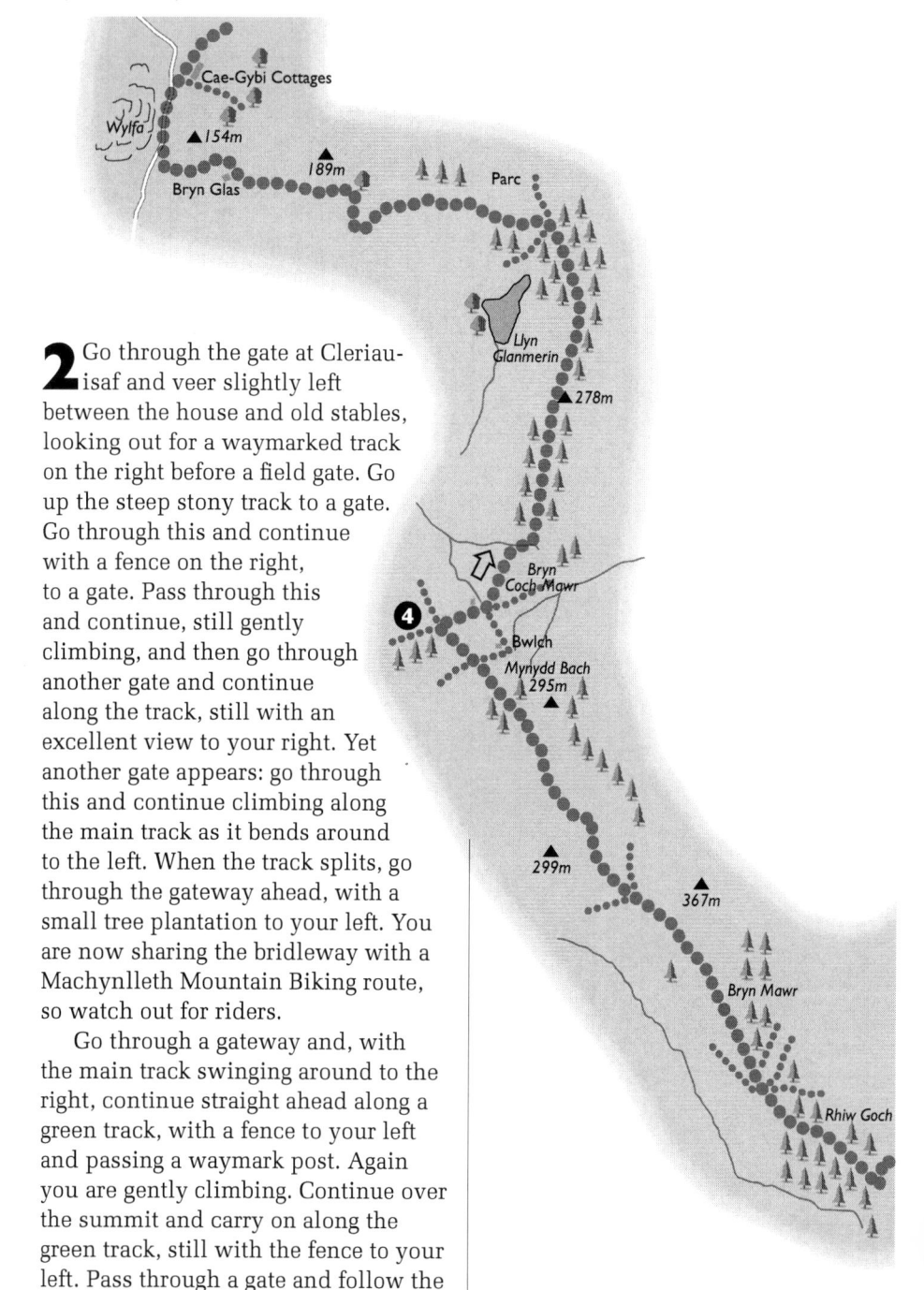

Glyndŵr's Way

2 Go through the gate at Cleriau-isaf and veer slightly left between the house and old stables, looking out for a waymarked track on the right before a field gate. Go up the steep stony track to a gate. Go through this and continue with a fence on the right, to a gate. Pass through this and continue, still gently climbing, and then go through another gate and continue along the track, still with an excellent view to your right. Yet another gate appears: go through this and continue climbing along the main track as it bends around to the left. When the track splits, go through the gateway ahead, with a small tree plantation to your left. You are now sharing the bridleway with a Machynlleth Mountain Biking route, so watch out for riders.

Go through a gateway and, with the main track swinging around to the right, continue straight ahead along a green track, with a fence to your left and passing a waymark post. Again you are gently climbing. Continue over the summit and carry on along the green track, still with the fence to your left. Pass through a gate and follow the

9 • Aberhosan to Machynlleth

track into a forest plantation. When you reach a forest road, cross it and continue on down to a gate and stile ahead, and go through. Veer right along the track and soon take the right fork as waymarked. You pass a tidy stone barn to the left and carry on through a small gate ahead. Follow the track downhill to a waymark post and walk across a field in the general direction of the furthest white house on the hillside ahead. The track soon becomes clearer and swings to the left towards Talbontdrain. Pass through a gate and walk down the track. Ford a small stream and continue up the track. Go through a gate and pass the house at Talbontdrain to walk up to the road, where you turn right.

3 The road now climbs and swings to the left and then to the right. Turn off left, as waymarked, at the entrance to Llwyn-gwyn to follow the main Glyndŵr's Way path, which is signed to the left. Go through a gate and continue with a fence to your left to the next gate, which you go through and carry on ahead to yet another gate, which you also go through, and carry on climbing. When the main track swings around to the left, you carry on ahead as waymarked to reach a gate. Go through this and walk ahead, climbing quite steeply now up a much eroded track, following the waymark posts. You climb very steeply up to a fenced area of felled forest, and turn left at the top to walk with the fence

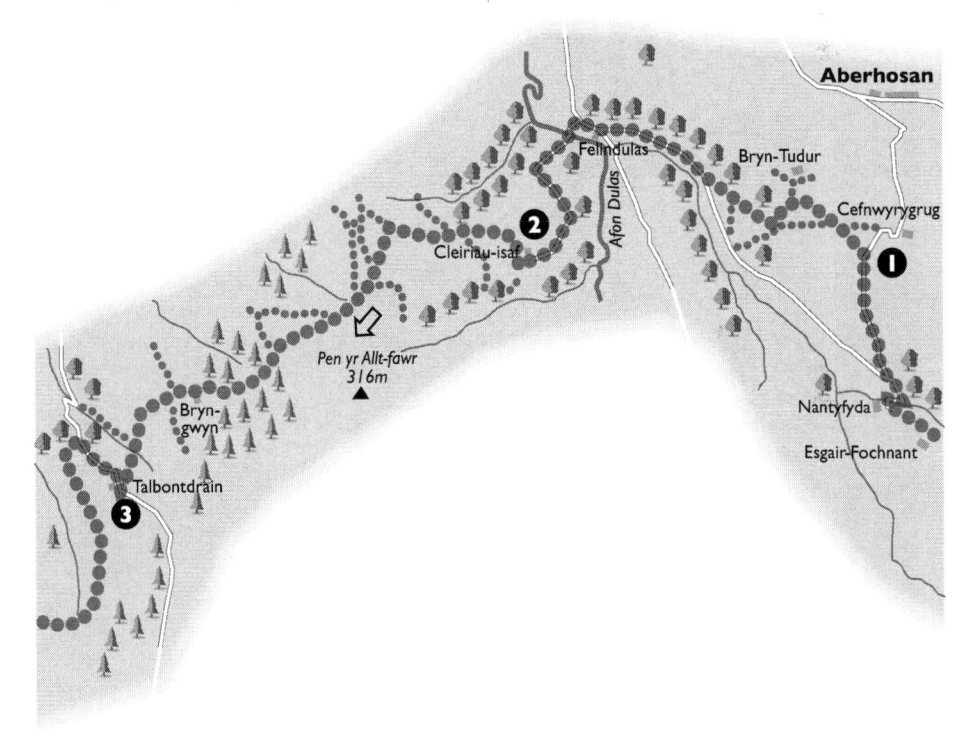

Glyndŵr's Way

on your right. *The views are stunning: a panorama of hills stretching north.* At the top of the track go through a gate and turn right. You have now once again joined one of the Machynlleth Mountain Biking routes – *this time at a notorious section known as 'The Chute': a very steep and testing downhill section over loose rock and wet and slippery slate* – so, again, watch out (cyclists may approach you very quickly from behind here!).

As you emerge from the felled trees a track forks off to the right, but you continue ahead, as waymarked. Go through a gate and continue with the fence to your right, and a fine view over the valley to your left. Ignore the bridleway signed to the left, and carry on uphill. Now the track maintains its height as it traverses the hillside. You go through a gate and continue with a fence to your left. When the fence ends, continue ahead along the track, to the next gate. Go through the gate and continue. Pass through a series of gates and continue along the track through forestry.

4 You reach a T junction where you turn right and take the gate to the left, to follow the green path (ignoring the gate to the right). Continue along the green path as it meanders downhill. Look-out for a waymark post, where you turn sharp left to climb uphill along a track which then swings around to the right, over a large patch of exposed rock, and continues uphill. Ignore a faint path which breaks away to the left and carry on uphill. You reach a gate and go through it. Now follow the clear track ahead. You pass several waymark posts on your left as you just continue ahead along the track. You reach a waymark post as you join another track and fork left. When the track dog-legs, look out for a waymark post which directs you to continue directly ahead.

The track now gently twists and turns, following a new track through felled forestry to eventually reach a couple of hundred yards of mature forestry and then a gate. Go though and follow the waymarked path ahead –*with superb views over the Dyfi Valley, a lone aero-generator prominent on a hilltop ahead, and Llyn Glanmerin below you to the left.* You now follow a clear path uphill and through bracken. Carry on ahead to a gate. Go through and follow the clear track downhill, with Machynlleth now in full view ahead, spread over the valley floor. Pass a waymark post and continue. When

9 • Aberhosan to Machynlleth

Cae-Gybi Cottages

you reach two gates ahead, go through the left-hand one and continue along the track. After about 50 yards you join another rough track, and continue ahead as waymarked. Pass Bryn-glas and, after about 100 yards, veer left to a gate. Go through and continue. The track descends through woods, swings around to the right and goes through a gate to join a road, where you continue ahead.

As the road descends and veers to the left, follow the track straight ahead. Ignore a gate to your right and continue ahead towards Machynlleth. Cross the track below Cae-Gybi Cottages and carry on downhill. You pass through a kissing-gate and continue along a defined path, which is quite steep and slippery. Carefully descend the Roman Steps, carved from the living slate (*but perhaps not by the Romans*) and very slippery when wet, to reach

another kissing-gate. Go through and walk ahead towards the road. Just before you reach the road, turn right through gates to enter The Plas (or you can leave the official route to join the road and turn right to walk to the clock-tower, and then turn right again to see most of the shops in the town). Now follow the track as waymarked, eventually passing in front of The Plas, by the commemorative (but sadly quite ugly) Glyndŵr stone. Veer right in front of the Bro Ddyfi Leisure Centre and follow the path as waymarked to eventually pass through wrought iron gates to reach the Owain Glyndŵr building in Maengwyn Street.

The handsome market town of Machynlleth marks the lowest crossing on the Afon Dyfi, so it is in a way almost a coastal town – in fact spring tides claw their way up the river as far as Pennal, once a Roman settlement,

49

just a couple of miles below the Dyfi Bridge. It is geographically pretty much at the centre of Wales and, with due regard to Cardiff, as fair a place as you could imagine for its capital.

This point was not wasted on Owain Glyndŵr, who did indeed make the town his capital in 1404, when he had himself crowned King of a free Wales at the Parliament House in Maengwyn Street (it has been rebuilt since then). A memorial, which you passed outside Plas Machynlleth, was ceremonially uncovered on 16 September 2000, marking 600 years since the start of his short-lived and ultimately unsuccessful revolt against the English Crown. Royal House, a stone's throw from the clock-tower, is said to be where Owain Glyndŵr resided when he held his parliament in Machynlleth – it is now a delicatessen and café. Dafydd Gam was imprisoned in a cellar here after he attempted to assassinate Owain. It took the name Royal House after Charles I stayed there in 1644 on a journey to Chester. An informal local 'parliament' was held from the 1920s to the 1940s in William Lewis' saddler's shop behind the town clock. The elders of the town debated local, national and international affairs, sitting on benches and boxes in a semi-circle in order of seniority. Meanwhile the saddler continued to stitch his leatherwork.

Try to find time to visit The Tabernacl Museum of Modern Art, Wales, which has fine exhibition spaces, with free admission. The adjacent auditorium has excellent acoustics and seating for 400 people, and there are performances from visiting musicians, as well as a truly splendid festival in late August, when many well-known performers are featured. Events range from recitals for children to jazz, and a lively Fringe provides further variety. Purchased by Andrew Lambert in 1984, The Tabernacl opened as simply a beautiful auditorium in 1986. Much work followed and eventually buildings next door were taken over and converted into an art gallery. Its expansion continues, with the old tannery soon to be incorporated.

At the other end of Machynlleth is Y Plas (you passed this as you entered the town), which was until 1948 the country seat of the Marquis of Londonderry. There are often exhibitions here, and it has a very pleassant tea room.

Having seen the sights of Machynlleth you might feel you need some refreshment. The town has a wide choice of pubs, inns and cafés, the most imposing of these being The Wynnstay in Maengwyn Street. It is a comfortable, friendly and welcoming hotel, visited by Lloyd George amongst others, with excellent accommodation, hospitable bars with a choice of real ales, and an outstanding chef. Machynlleth was recently lauded as one of the top 32 places in Britain 'not to be missed'. It is truly remarkable that this compact little town, right in the heart of rural Wales, has become a vibrant and stylish centre not only of local life, but of art, culture, cycling and walking. Machynlleth is an excellent place to break your journey for a day or two, to rest, recuperate and enjoy its attractions.

10 • MACHYNLLETH to CEMMAES ROAD
8¾ miles

From the Owain Glyndŵr building in Machynlleth walk along Maengwyn Street in the direction of Newtown. When you reach the Bro Dyfi Community Hospital on the left, turn right as signed towards Dylife and walk along Treowain, passing the Health Centre and the Treowain Enterprise Park. Continue ahead along the road as you pass the last house on the left and begin gently climbing. Cross a cattle grid and follow the road as it traverses the golf course. *On your left is a small obelisk in an enclosure: it is part of the Ordnance Surveys' Global Positioning System.* You leave the golf course over a second cattle grid and follow the road as it swings to the right by a waymark post. Stay on the road as you enter the village of Forge, turning left and then right over the bridge (do not go straight ahead), passing a telephone kiosk and staying on the road, which you are sharing with National Cycle Route 8. *Forge once supported five fulling mills, or pandys, the last of which closed in 1937, and there was at one time a small electricity generating station by Dolgau farm, set up in 1931. The village has been famous amongst beekeepers for many years, thanks to the efforts of Alfred Evans, who regularly broadcast on the subject.*

The Clock Tower, Machynlleth

Glyndŵr's Way

2 Pass the house 'Dolhan' on the right and turn left, as signposted, along a lane and soon, as you gently climb, a very pretty view opens to the north-west. When the lane dips slightly and passes under electricity cables before bending to the left, you turn right to follow a track. Continue to a gate, go through and continue to the gate into Penrhos-bach farmyard. Do not go through this but turn right and walk, with the fence on your left,

adjoining buildings are used for holiday accommodation. When you reach the main road, turn right. *The village of Penegoes, harrassed by the main road, has ancient connections with the Princes of Powys: nearby Dolguog is associated with the fortress, long since disappeared, of Owain Cyfeiliog, the ruler and poet who died in 1197. A short distance along the road towards Machynlleth you will find the church, beyond which is a*

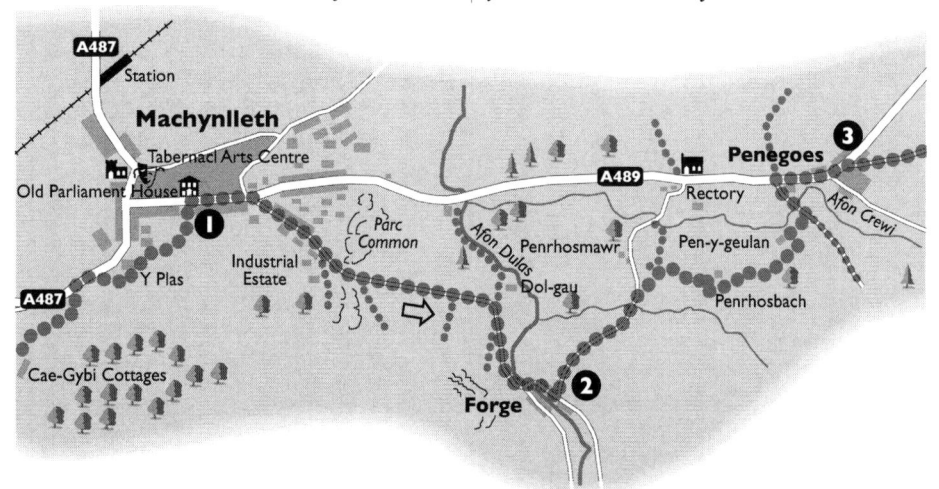

to a stile. Cross this and continue ahead to a waymark post. Keeping the hedge-line to your left carry on to the stile ahead. Cross this, initially keeping electricity posts to your left to stay above the badger sets then, at the summit, veer towards the next electricity post ahead. Now drop down the hill to a stony track, where you turn left. Pass through a gate, then another and turn right along a farm road. Go through a gate, walk down to a road and turn left as signed.

Cross a bridge and pass the restored 17th century water mill, where the

grove of oaks where the head of Egeos, the Celtic saint who gave his name to the village (Pen-egoes – head of egoes) is said to be buried. The rectory was the birthplace of Richard Wilson (1714-82), a landscape artist, and was later visited by Felicia Dorothea Hemans (1793-1835) who wrote the much abused poem Casabianca, containing the line: 'The boy stood on the burning deck'. She came here to visit her brother-in-law, who was rector. Just over the hedge opposite, and right by the main road, is an ancient healing well.

10 • Machynlleth to Cemmaes Road

3 Walk along the road, ignoring the first turning to the right and then, after 50 yards, forking right along a lane by houses and continuing out of the village. Fork right by Maesperthi, as directed by the waymark post, to walk up a rougher track towards Maesllwyni. When a farm track joins from the right, continue ahead to reach a gate. Go through and carry on along the track to go through another gate and continue gently uphill. You are now progressing up a cwm, with a stream down to your right and a fine view over Penegoes behind you, against a backdrop of the rolling hills of the Dyfi Valley. Still climbing, you pass a small stand of conifers on the right and reach a gate: go through and continue ahead. Eventually you reach two gates. Take the left-hand gate and turn sharp left to climb steeply uphill, with a fence to your left. Initially the climb is quite hard work, but the summit is soon reached and then you are gently descending, with a very fine view over the Dyfi Valley. The tiny village directly ahead and across the river is Llanwrin, where the early English style St Gwrin's church has a handsome rood screen and some stained glass dating from 1461. The original church was originally dedicated to the saints Ust and Dyfrig, who came here from Brittany in Ad 516. Canon Silvan Evans lived in the rectory from 1876 to 1903. He compiled the Welsh dictionary and was the first Welsh lecturer at Aberystwyh University.

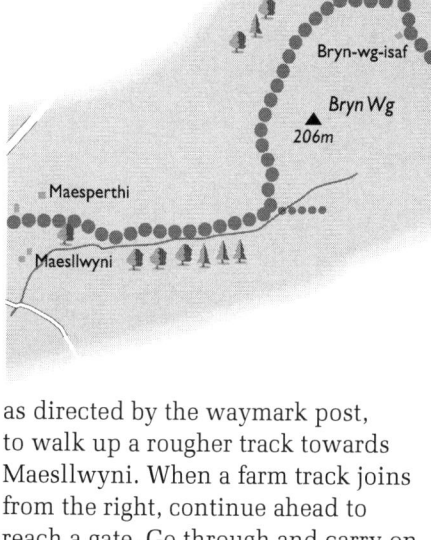

You reach a very large ladder-stile, beneath which two fences cross. Climb this and now walk with the fence to your right through rough ground, looking out for the waymark post ahead. When you reach it, continue, still with the fence to your right, towards the next post, and still with a magnificent view over the valley. Carry on ahead, leaving the bracken and gorse behind for a while, and then entering another patch of it.

Eventually a waymark post appears

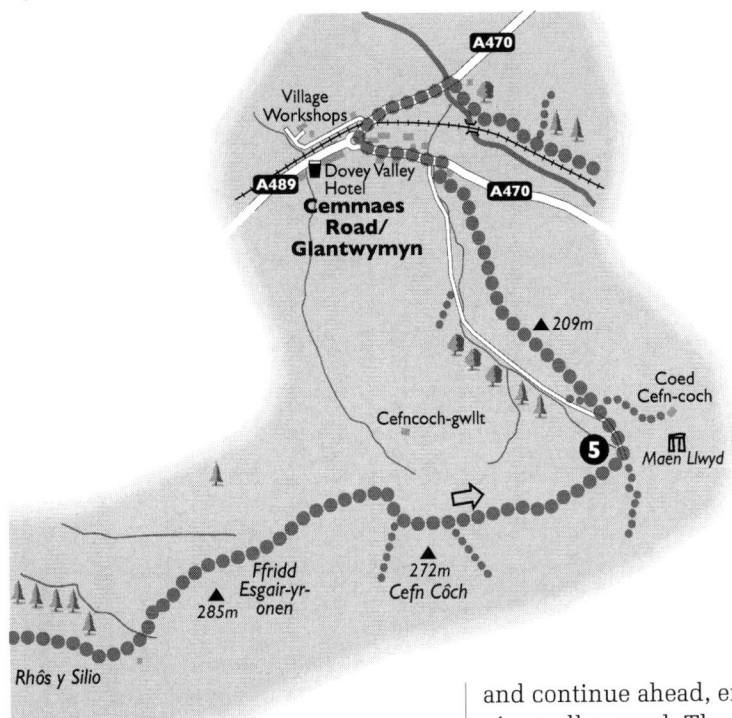

amidst more bracken, and you are directed to veer right. When the fence veers slightly right, continue as directed by the waymark post, dipping steeply down to find a gate, which is well hidden by the bracken during the summer. Go through this and climb up to another waymark post. Walk ahead, with the fence still to your right. As you cross a farm track look for a waymark post which directs you to cross a stile and veer left along a rough path through more bracken, above a little cwm to the right. Very soon you reach a waymark post, where you turn right at a path junction. *Below you and ahead is the village of Abercegir, nestling at a junction of three steep valleys.* Cross a tiny stream and continue ahead, enjoying stunning views all around. The narrow path you are following dips into a cwm and then climbs to a waymark post. Carry on, with a fence to your right as you gradually descend the hillside. Continue ahead as waymarked (do not go uphill). *Below you, to the left, is Factory Isaf, a former flannel factory.* Follow the path as it zig-zags downhill to a small gate, which you go through to walk along a hedged lane. When this joins a farm track by a cattle grid and a waymark post, continue ahead. Turn left off the track as waymarked, to walk to the left of Yr Hen Felin (very comfortable B&B, 01650 511818), cross a bridge and follow the path to the right – *which gives you a fine view of the remains of the water wheel* – before you reach the road in the village centre.

10 • Machynlleth to Cemmaes Road

On the way to Forge

4 Turn left and walk along the road for about 50 yards to a junction, where you turn sharp right by Top y Pentre and walk along the road, gently climbing to leave Abercegir. Now look out for a track which joins from the left and turn sharp left here, and follow this as it climbs gently uphill and swings to the right. When you approach the top of the track, turn left through a small gate, then turn right and walk with the fence to your right. Ignore the first, metal, gate on your right and walk up to the second, wooden, gate in the top right-hand field corner, and go through as waymarked. Now walk uphill with a wall to your left, passing through a gate and enjoying a fine view to your left beyond the wall. Ignore a field gate to your left and continue ahead through a gap in the hedge. Go through a small wooden gate and carry on, still climbing with the fence and hedge to your left. Go through a small wooden gate and veer slightly right around the hill, still climbing. *The view is now more expansive, with Llanwrin nestling in the Dyfi Valley with a single aero-generator on the hill behind it.*

You come to a wooden gate in a stone wall. Go through and walk half-left uphill, gradually leaving the wall away to your left as you again swing around the hill. Soon you join a green farm road coming in from the right, and you now follow this, still climbing with the summit of Rhôs y Silio up to your right. The track passes through a broken gateway as you carry on ahead, still climbing. *To the north the summit of Cadair Idris has now become visible, and to the north-east the competing summit of Aran Fawddwy is also prominent.*

The track eventually swings slightly right and peters out in a field: you continue ahead to a gate, and go

55

through and veer slightly left towards trees. Look out for the waymark post, which stands amongst the remnants of an old hedge line and, when you reach this, veer left as directed towards the next post, and carry on as signed, now with the summit of Aran Fawddwy on the horizon directly ahead.

Go between old gate posts and turn right to follow a fence to your right. Turn left to pass through another gate and walk ahead along a broad green track, with a fence to your left. *As you progress, look back for a view of the Afon Dyfi, a salmon and sea trout river, glistening in the sun. The track is delightful, carpeted with deep grass and carved into the high slope of Cefn Coch. Ahead is the Cemmaes Ridge, topped by a spread of large aero-generators which comprise the Cemmaes Wind Farm. The hills are speckled with sheep and patterned with mostly broken stone walls, and all is utter peace (especially at weekends,* *when the military jets are not flying).*

When you reach a gate go through it and continue, veering just slightly left across an open field and enjoying an opening view along the broad valley towards Dinas Mawddwy. The field is quite wet and marshy in places. Follow the waymarks towards a stone wall which joins your route from the left. Walk beside this towards a waymark post by a track. Join the track and turn right to walk uphill. Go through a gate and continue straight ahead towards a gate, which you go through and veer left, to walk with a low wall and a fence to your left.

When you reach a gate, go through and carry on with the wall still to your left, to reach yet another gate, Go through this gate to walk beside a now intact wall. When you reach two gates in the field corner, go through the left hand one to walk down a track. Pass a gate to your left and continue ahead. Pass through a gate to emerge at the

10 • Machynlleth to Cemmaes Road

They don't build them like this any more!

top of a lane, where you turn left.

About a mile south of here, along the track to your right, is the ancient settlement of Darowen, and tucked away in the Ffernant valley, a half-a-mile south-east of this village, is old Pwlliwrch, the hidden farm where some think Owain Glyndŵr may have ended his days. In the field ahead of you at the track junction is Maen Llwyd, one of two surviving stones of three which once marked an area of sanctuary around Darowen, and which aligns, through the churchyard and the other survivng stone, with one of the five summits of Pumlumon.

5 Walk downhill and, when the lane veers left, carry on ahead, going through a gate on your right. Maintain your direction across the field to reach a gate in the fence ahead. Go through and carry on to the next gate, which you go through, then continue over the brow of the hill, keeping the steep valley to your left, to reach another gate. Go through this and carry on ahead down towards Cemmaes Road. As you approach a fence, and just before a small enclosure, look to your right to see a gate. Go through this and then turn left to descend along a track – *passing a last resting place for veteran tractors, gracefully and picturesquely decaying*. Go through a gate and follow the fence to a small wooden gate on the right. Go through this and walk down to another gate.

Go through and turn left into the village where there is a post office, and the Tafarn y Dyfi. This is a remarkable and historic real ale pub with a very handsome and unspoiled traditional bar, unaltered since 1913, where a local real ale can be enjoyed, along with bar snacks. There is an open fire from Autumn to Spring. (01650 511335, open daily 18.00-23.00).

Glyndŵr's Way

11 • CEMMAES ROAD to LLANBRYNMAIR
6¾ miles

From the roundabout in Cemmaes Road walk along the road towards Dolgellau, initially crossing over the railway, and then the Afon Twymyn, and then turning immediately sharp right through a gate and continuing along a drive, passing a very fine brick railway arch over the river, to your right. Continue climbing gently uphill, with tall trees on your left. Go through the next gate and carry on, with scattered stands of trees on your left, and the railway and the steep river valley to your right, with the main road thankfully well hidden amongst trees. When you reach a fork in the track, at a waymark post, go left and continue gently uphill. The track swings left and continues to gently climb, soon reaching a waymark post, where you turn left off the clear track to climb an extremely pleasant green track up the side of the hill. *Take a rest while you are climbing and look over your shoulder, where there are clear views of the hills to the south west.*

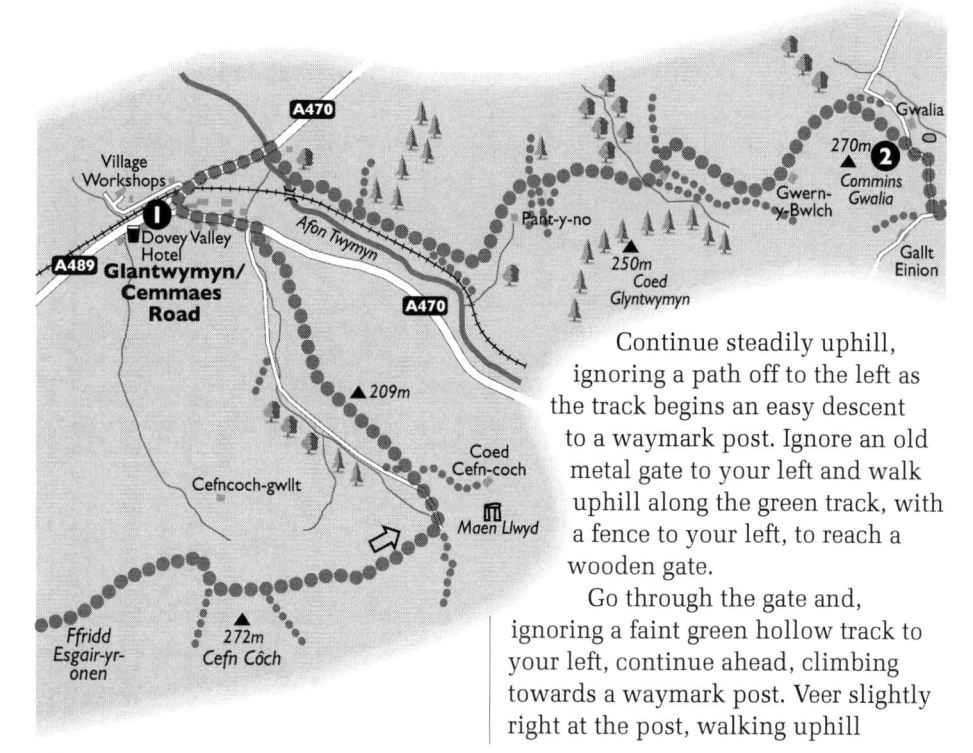

Continue steadily uphill, ignoring a path off to the left as the track begins an easy descent to a waymark post. Ignore an old metal gate to your left and walk uphill along the green track, with a fence to your left, to reach a wooden gate.

Go through the gate and, ignoring a faint green hollow track to your left, continue ahead, climbing towards a waymark post. Veer slightly right at the post, walking uphill

58

11 • Cemmaes Road to Llanbrynmair

towards a metal gate. Go through the gate and continue downhill to the next gate. Pass through this and carry on ahead to go through another gate and reach a waymark post, where you turn left along a clear track beneath a house on a small hill to your right. Continue uphill through a gate, passing a restored farm to your right and barns to your left, and turning left as waymarked. After about 20 yards you reach two gates. Go through the one on the left.

Now walk gently uphill – *enjoying fine views across the Dyfi Valley towards Mallwyd, which open to your left*. The track bends sharply right and continues through a gate, and on through a second gate gradually entering more open countryside, redolent of the moorlands traversed in previous sections further south. Go through a gateway as the track swings to the left, passing Gwern-y-Bwlch. Having climbed gently across a field to a gate, you go through and find the views now opening to your right. Go through the gate and carry on, keeping the fence to your left. Go through a gate and continue ahead, crossing rough ground but following a clear track towards a waymark post. *As the track swings to the right around the side of the hill there are splendid views ahead of Mynydd y Cemmaes, with the second-generation aero-generators just peeking over the ridge. The summit at the southern end is Moel Eiddew, 1486 feet high.* The track now begins its descent to the road, passing Gwalia down to your left, its chimney stack just visible through the trees. Eventually you reach a gate, which you go through to join the road.

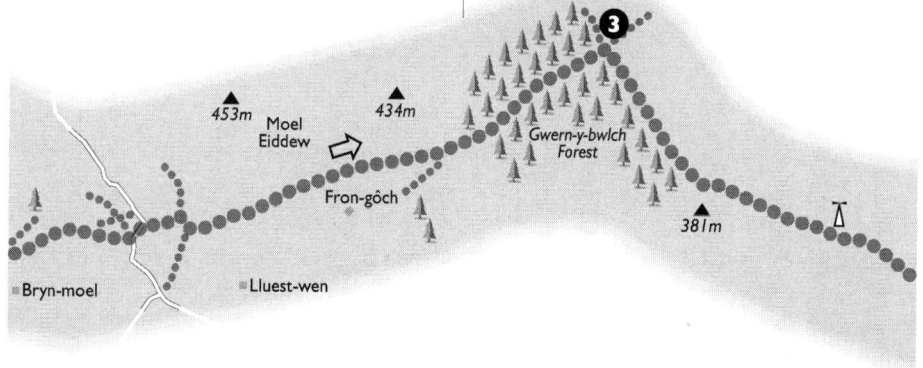

2 Continue ahead along this very quiet road as it at first swings gently right and continues to a much sharper right turn: here you turn sharp left, along a track, as waymarked. Carry on ahead along the track where the track from Bryn-moel joins from the right. After a gentle climb, a wooden gate appears ahead. Go through this and carry on ahead, keeping the fence on your left, along what is now a wide green track. Descend gently to a gate, go through and turn left along a narrow road. After 100 yards turn right, go through a gate which is set a little back from the road, and proceed ahead

59

Make sure you give them plenty of space .....

along a green track. As you climb, a fence joins your route to the right. Stay on the track as it bends to the right and continues climbing, now quite steeply. When your route splits, continue ahead as waymarked. Go through a gate and carry on, keeping the fence to your right. *There are now expansive views over the Twymyn Valley towards the summit of Corun y Ffridd.*

Eventually the undergrowth to your right clears and you can find your way into the hollow lane which follows the edge of the field, with the fence still to your right – *and absolutely splendid views beyond, beneath the ubiquitous buzzards.* When you reach a gate, go through and continue ahead. Go through another two gates above Fron-gôch and carry on along the track, with a large forestry plantation looming ahead. Another gate is passed as you approach the trees, with the fence to your right, and enter a plantation through a small wooden gate.

You are now in Gwern-y-bwlch Forest – *a board to your left indicates three waymarked walks should you feel the need for a diversion* – where Glyndŵr's Way initially descends to a modest clearing and joins a forest road. Walk to the left as waymarked, climbing very gently uphill and now following a pleasant forest road. It's gentle uphill walking, hardly noticeable on the smooth surface. The track climbs to a point where it swings away left – just before here look out for a waymark post on the right, which directs you to fork off onto a lesser path, which soon brings you to a small wooden gate at the edge of what was a plantation.

11 • Cemmaes Road to Llanbrynmair

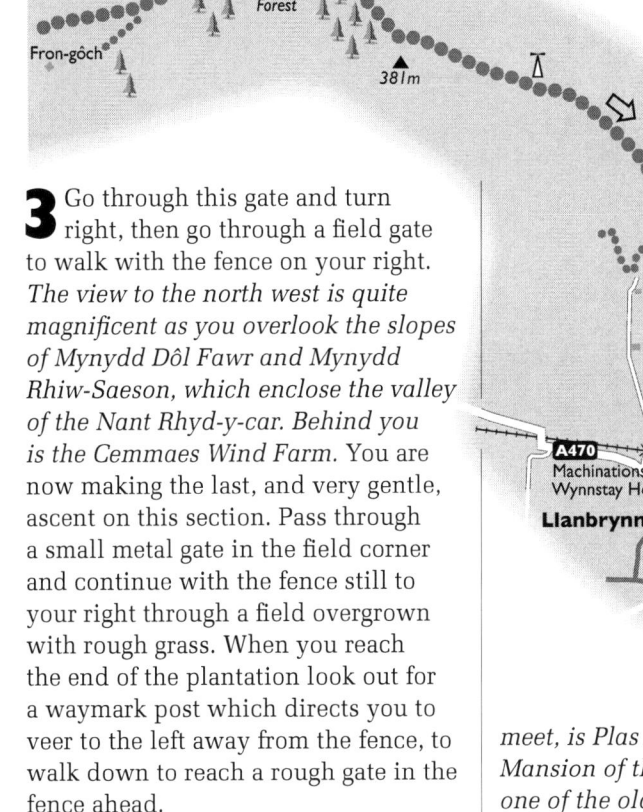

3 Go through this gate and turn right, then go through a field gate to walk with the fence on your right. *The view to the north west is quite magnificent as you overlook the slopes of Mynydd Dôl Fawr and Mynydd Rhiw-Saeson, which enclose the valley of the Nant Rhyd-y-car. Behind you is the Cemmaes Wind Farm.* You are now making the last, and very gentle, ascent on this section. Pass through a small metal gate in the field corner and continue with the fence still to your right through a field overgrown with rough grass. When you reach the end of the plantation look out for a waymark post which directs you to veer to the left away from the fence, to walk down to reach a rough gate in the fence ahead.

Go through this and continue ahead as a transmitter pylon comes into view. Walk towards the right hand side of this, following the brow of the hill. You are now presented with a stunning panorama as you face the valley towards Talerddig, soon passing through the gate beside the transmitter and continuing downhill, along a track with a fence to your left. *To the north-east, at the point where two valleys meet, is Plas Rhiw Saeson ('the Mansion of the Hill of the English'), one of the oldest inhabited houses in the area, dating from the 11th century. This area has a tradition of attracting great poets, and many stayed at Rhiw Saeson. Notable amongst them was Richard Davies, who was born in 1833 and took the bardic name of Mynyddog. He wrote 'Sospan Fach' amongst others. Another famous son was Iorwerth C Peate, who became first curator of the Welsh Folk Museum at St Fagan's, Cardiff.*

The exhibition, Machinations

4 The track levels as you approach a gate, which you pass through and continue ahead to reach the concrete road leading to Bryn-aire-uchaf. Veer right to gate beside a shed. Walk along the side of the shed to the next field gate, which you go through to continue to the next field gate. Continue down the meadow to a pedestrian gate in a hedgeline, then on down the meadow to a gated footbridge. Cross this and walk, with the fence to your left, to a pedestrian gate, which you go through and continue following the fence line. Turn sharp right at a waymark post. Walk down the field to another post, where you turn right to reach a pedestrian gate in a fence. Go through this and walk down to a stone track. At the end of the track turn left at a waymark post and walk down the farm road. Cross the river and continue to the Pandy road, where you turn right. If you continue along the road, ignoring the Glyndŵr's Way waymark and kissing gate to your left, you will reach Llanbrynmair.

Here you will find the Wynnstay Hotel (real ale, food and accommodation – 01650 521431), a post office and shop, and the quite unique Machinations Museum of Mechanical Magic exhibition and café. *This museum contains wonderful and fascinating hand-made models, continuing the 17th century Black Forest tradition of clocks featuring mechanical scenes through to the classic age of automata in 19th century France. Beautifully constructed, they reflect the work of two local village craftsmen, Eric Williamson and Peter Markey, whose 'Timberkits' are sold here. There is also an excellent wholefood café and a shop. It is open every day.*

A thinker, but not a farmer

Llanbrynmair has long been known for the numbers of eminent people – artists, writers, politicians – who have grown up in the surrounding hills. Many have emigrated to America, prompting the Rev. Samuel Roberts, a Congregational minister in the village and known affectionately as 'SR', to comment in 1857 in a letter from Cincinnati: 'Of the people born in Llanbrynmair in the last fifty years there are more now living in America than in Llanbrynmair'.

This emigration was more often than not forced upon those who left by unscrupulous landowners in Wales. William Jones described the reasons in 1790: 'The hardships which the poor inhabitants of this barren country suffer by the Insatiable Avarice of the Landowners, have affected my feelings so, that I had determined to write to London to get Intelligence of some proprietor of uncultivated land in America in order to offer my services to concert a Plan for removing such of my countrymen as have spirit enough to leave their Aegyptian Taskmasters and try their fortune on the other side of the Atlantic'.

SR established a company in 1856 which purchased 100,000 acres of land in Tennessee in order to establish a Welsh settlement there. Unfortunately a series of disputes rendered the scheme unworkable, and the state's involvement with slavery created a moral dilemma for him. Humphrey and Sarah Roberts wrote from Ohio in 1861: 'The Welsh in America have worshiped (sic) Samuel Roberts, Llanbrynmair, like Great Diana of Ephesus. He sent a letter here to the North recently, saying that he had swallowed the accursed doctrine of the slave dealers in Tennessee. He says in his letter that the people of the South are more noble and righteous than the people of the North, and that the people of the North are to blame for the conflict. Oh! servant of the enemy and a wolf in sheep's clothing! If he came with his letter, the preachers of the North would give him the coat of tar and feathers which he deserves. Now he is caught in his own trap. It is supposed that he wrote against slavery in Wales and this rises against him now. Enough of the wretch!'

SR was stung by this wholly untrue criticism, and returned to Liverpool in 1867 during the American Civil War, only to return to America in 1870 in an attempt to sell the land. Part of the failure of this venture was attributed to the fact that SR was a progressive, a preacher, a thinker, a writer and a reformer – but not a farmer.

Glyndŵr's Way

12• LLANBRYNMAIR to LLANGADFAN
10¼ miles

If you are starting from the village of Llanbrynmair walk along the minor road to the left of the Wynnstay Arms, signed to Pandy. Continue under the very large stone railway arch, looking out for a signed kissing gate on the right. If you are continuing without visiting Llanbrynmair, look for the signed kissing gate. Go through. When you reach the kissing gate on the left, go through it and follow the track uphill, soon passing through two gates. After the second gate turn immediately right, leaving the track to cross over a small plank bridge and a gate. Now walk initially with the fence to your left, then veer gradually away, ignoring a gate and crossing a stile ahead, just beyond a railway sleeper bridge over a ditch. Continue ahead, still with the fence to your left, go through a gate, and then over a footbridge, and veer left. Look out for a waymark post, and walk towards it, before veering left towards a conspicuous large tree. Go

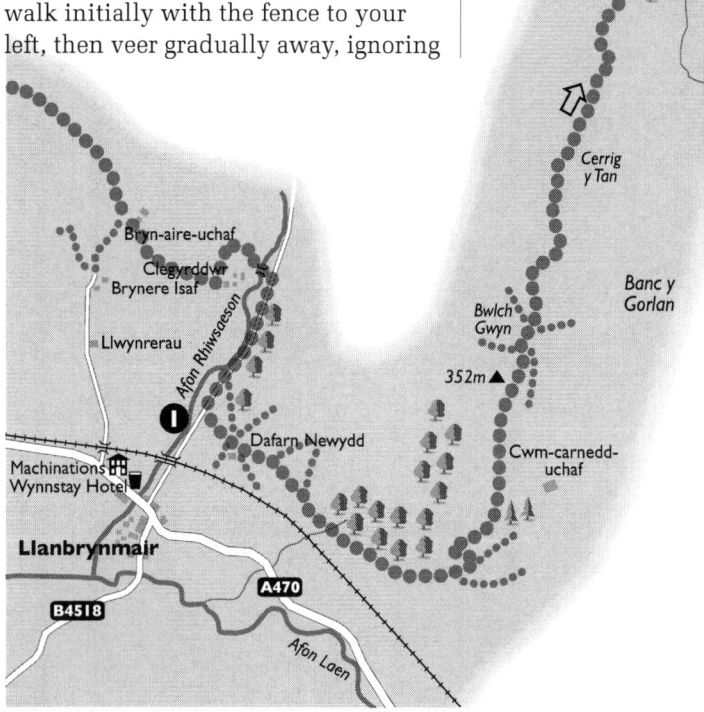

64

12 • Llanbrynmair to Llangadfan

through a gate beneath the tree and turn left, to walk uphill, with a large gully to your left. As you climb, look out for a waymark post which directs you to veer to the right away from the gully. As you approach a line of hefty old trees look out for a waymark post, which directs you to take the left hand and grassy track up the hill, again veering left and still climbing.

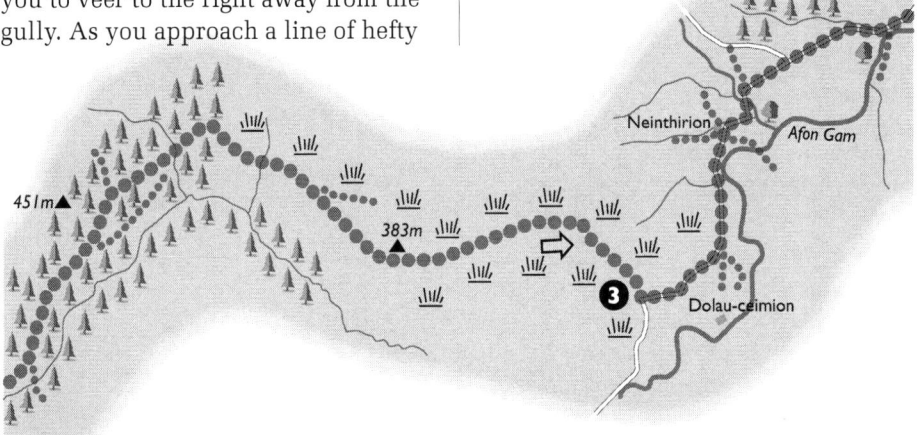

Go through a gate and continue along the green track. *The main road is at last out of sight and the views to your right are quite dramatic.* As the track veers left you reach two waymark posts in quick succession: at the second turn sharp left to follow the rough green track up the hill to reach a fence, where you turn right, to continue with the fence and wall to your left – *now enjoying a spectacular view over Llanbrynmair, and both the Pennant and Dyfi Valleys.*

Soon the track veers away from the wall and you continue, following it uphill. Continue ahead, still climbing as a fence joins from the right. Cross a stile beside a gate and carry on ahead across a field following the very slight indentation which was once a track.

Cross a stile and continue ahead.

As you come off the shoulder of this mountain look for a stile in the wall ahead. Cross this and veer right to pick up a clear green track. Follow this, skirting the western side of Banc y Gorlan along an old track-way – *enjoying quite superb views towards Mynydd Rhiw-Saeson.* When a track joins from the left, continue ahead as indicated on the waymark post. You reach a gate ahead (ignore the gate over to your left), which you go through and continue along the clear track. *Looking towards the south-west, you can now enjoy an absolutely splendid view of the Pennant Valley, which culminates at Dylife, passed earlier on Glyndŵr's Way.* Now follow the clear route over Cerrig y Tan. As the track veers slightly to the right you reach a wooden gate. Go through and continue, now with the fence to your left, towards another gate.

Glyndŵr's Way

2 Go through the gate and continue ahead along the clear track to enter the forestry through a gate. Now follow the track, eventually being reassured by a waymark post. When you reach a T-junction, turn left and carry on, keeping a careful watch for a waymark post to your right, which appears shortly after views begin to open on the right. When you reach this waymark, fork right off the main forest road down a lesser, but at this point clear, track. When this track divides, veer right as directed by the waymark post. Cross a small ditch and carry on ahead, with the track gradually narrowing. Soon you are sharing your route with a ditch, so take great care. Finally you cross this ditch to emerge at a gate.

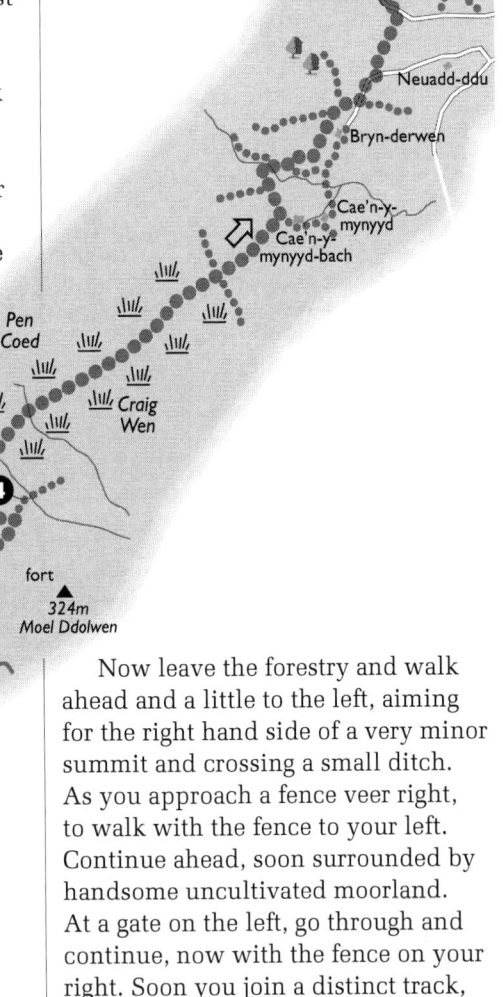

Now leave the forestry and walk ahead and a little to the left, aiming for the right hand side of a very minor summit and crossing a small ditch. As you approach a fence veer right, to walk with the fence to your left. Continue ahead, soon surrounded by handsome uncultivated moorland. At a gate on the left, go through and continue, now with the fence on your right. Soon you join a distinct track, which you follow downhill, enjoying

12 • Llanbrynmair to Llangadfan

extensive views of the valley and moorland ahead. Stay on the track as it swings to the right and continues its steady descent, still with the fence to the right. Pass through a gate and continue, descending to join a tarmac lane, where you turn left.

3 Stay on this road, which shares the valley with the Afon Gam, ignoring a track off to the right by a cattle grid sign. Pass Neinthirion, with a chapel next door, and stay on the road, crossing the Afon Cannon. When the road swings right at Dolwen, continue ahead as signed. Cross the foot bridge, which is to the left of a vehicle bridge, opposite Dolwen and pass through two gates to leave the farmyard and walk along a track between stone walls. When you reach two gates side-by-side, pass through the left hand one and continue along the track, climbing steadily. Pass through a gate and carry on along a beautiful tree-lined lane. Pass through another gate and continue ahead, joining a track which comes in from the right, and follow this, with a fence and trees on the left,

until you reach a gate on the left. Go through this and walk along the track. Follow this when it swings left and then right, enjoying superb views.

4 Go through a gate and carry on ahead looking out for short waymark posts with yellow tops which mark your route over Pen Coed Common through the tussocks of rough grazing. You begin your descent of Pen Coed, walking from post to post, picking your way around the boggy patches and admiring some attractive ponies which roam up here. Continue your descent, veering to the right looking out for a fence and then keeping parallel to this. When your descent steepens veer away from the fence and around to the left. Look out for a footbridge, close to a fence at the bottom of the hill. Walk towards this, cross it, cross the attached stile and turn sharp right heading for a waymark post. Continue towards a small stone sheep pen but, just before it, swing left up a rocky track towards a waymark post. At the waymark post take a sharp left as directed and walk up the hedge line towards another waymark post, where you turn right. Continue as directed to reach another waymark post above a house. Veer left to walk with a fence, and the house, over to your right. Follow the fence until you reach a gate. Go through and walk ahead towards a finger post on the far side of the field. Go through a gate by the post to join a lane and turn left.

Just after the lane swings to the right and gently descends, go through a gate on the left and walk ahead to a second stile, which you cross. Pick your way across a roughly felled area of what was once woodland and look for a stile in the bottom right hand corner. Cross a ditch, cross the stile and veer right towards a stile and a waymark post at the far side of the next rough and wet field. Cross the stile and turn left to walk along a lane.

After about 50 yards turn right through a gate and follow a track with a hedge to the left to approach Bryncyrch. You can now see Llangadfan ahead. Pass the farm to your right and continue through a gate and turn left. Continue, and when you reach a T-junction, turn right. Just after the road swings to the right, turn left to cross a footbridge over the Afon Banwy, and pass a chapel to reach the main road at Llangadfan. The excellent Cann Office Hotel (01938 820202), which serves food, and real ale in a plain and charming public bar, and offers accommodation, is just a short distance to the right.

13 • LLANGADFAN to LLANWDDYN
6½ miles

Llangadfan takes its name from the Celtic Saint Cadfan, who in the 6th century travelled to Wales from Brittany. A dedicated well lies just to the south – this was saved from being covered by a new road when the Rev. Griffith Howell (1839-63) stepped in. Cadfan was later to become the first Abbot of Bardsey Island. Just along the main road to the south is the handsome Cann Office Hotel, its name thought to derive from Cae'n y ffos, which means a fortified enclosure. This ancient earthwork was built in the 12th century in what is now the hotel's back garden. Cross the main A458 road and continue ahead along a lane, with a red-brick chapel to your left and a handsome stone barn to your right. Continue up the lane, passing an unusual angular wooden house on your left.

When you reach the entrance to Blowty, turn left, go through the gate and walk along the lane until you reach a stile on the right. Cross this and walk around the edge of the field, keeping the hedge to your right. Cross a stile ahead and continue straight across a field to reach another stile. Cross this, cross the track and climb the stile opposite, to walk with trees to your right. Maintain your direction when the trees finish to reach a stile on the far side. Cross this and continue along a long, narrow field. Go through a gate at the far end and carry on with a fence and a hedge to your left. Descend to the corner of the field, cross a stile and a footbridge and carry on, now with the hedge to your right. Climb up the hill, pass through a gate to the right of some sheds to reach a stile. Cross this to join the road and continue ahead, passing Bryngwalia and then Pant-gwyn. When you reach a T junction, continue ahead, going through a gate and walking with the fence on your left, beyond which there is a pleasant but undramatic view towards Foel. *The track is wide enough to have been a drover's road, a network of routes used until the end of the 19th century to bring livestock from the Welsh hills to the markets of London.* Go through a gate and continue ahead, now with the fence and hedge to your right. Carry on gently downhill and, when the fence to your right ends, continue ahead along an old hollow lane with trees, and the remains of a wall, to your left. This track is at times quite boggy.

The track now climbs along a hedged lane to pass through a gate. You maintain your direction along this enclosed and quite overgrown track, picking your way through thistles and nettles. Go though a gate and continue along the edge of a field, with the fence to your left. Walk uphill and pass through a gate to join a road.

Glyndŵr's Way

2 Turn left, walk ahead for 15 yards and then turn right along a clear, wide, waymarked forest track, climbing gently. When you reach a clear forest road, turn left as waymarked. *After a short while conifers to your left clear to give a wonderful open panoramic view of the Banwy Valley, with gentle rolling hills and mountains beyond. The main summit to the south west is Pen Coed, rising to 1181 feet.* Follow the track as it swings gently to the right and passes a waymark post. Once again you are walking enclosed amidst conifers. Pass a waymark post and continue ahead as directed. A second post shortly after performs the same function. Then at last Glyndŵr's Way has shed, at least for a while, its preoccupation with waymarks, changes of direction, gates, stiles and junctions and you can relax and just follow a clear track, with little to distract you apart from the fine view at Pren Croes. Another waymark post confirms you are not lost as you press on, climbing gently.

At a cross-tracks, continue slightly right and ahead to reach a more formally arranged junction of five tracks, where you press on ahead and to the right downhill as signposted and waymarked. When the main forest road swings around to the right, you continue ahead down a waymarked, hollow lane. Soon you descend a small dingle amidst tall mature conifers, with the sound of a tumbling stream down to your

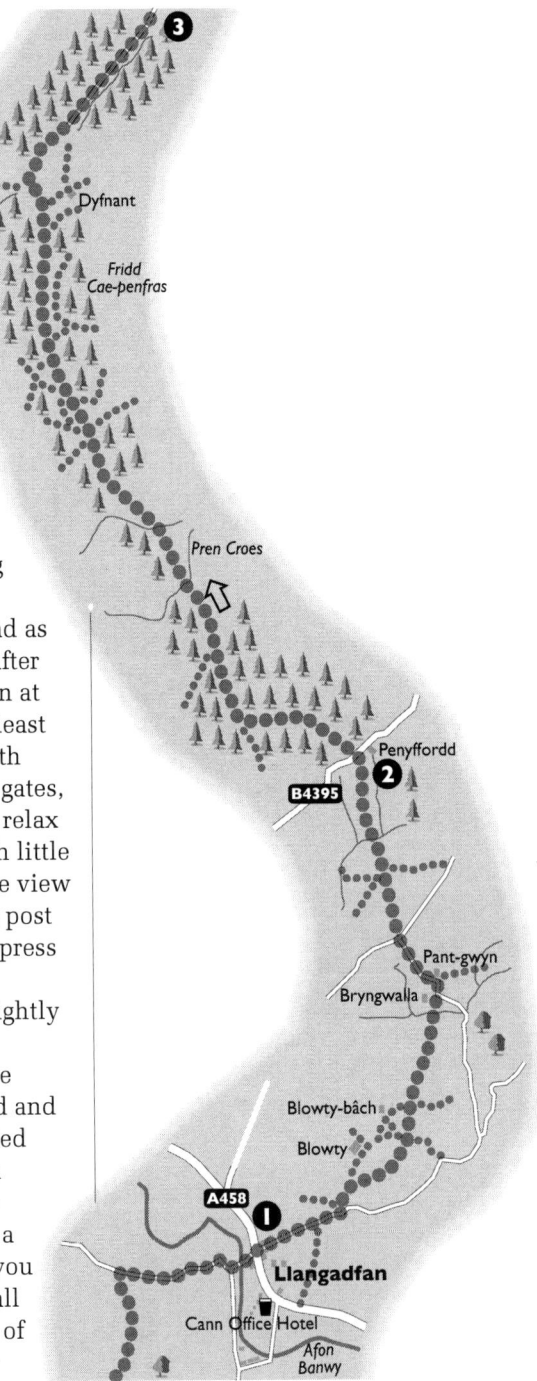

13 • Llangadfan to Llanwddyn

right. Walk straight across the bend of a forest road and continue down to a gate, and go through. Continue ahead with the fence, and trees, on your left. Pass a waymarked gateway and carry on ahead, then when the track bends to the right and a stream crosses, ignore the two gates ahead and continue downhill along the track. The going is quite rough here, as a stream shares the lane, and the surface is comprised of small uneven boulders.

Descend to a stream where there is a wooden bridge with a gate, and cross it. Continue ahead along the clear track and, when you reach a lane, turn right as signed. You are now walking with rough tarmac underfoot, along the side of a valley and amidst trees, with a stream somewhere down to your right. A quite substantial hedge eventually replaces the forest to your right – *giving an occasional glimpse of the fine view down towards Parc Llwydiarth.* Then at last the hedge drops away and the views open. When a forest track forks to the left, ignore it and continue ahead as a second track, from Maesdyfnant, joins from the right.

3 Maintain your direction along what is now a clear road. You descend to pass the entrance to The Lake Vyrnwy Holiday Home Park, then cross a bridge and turn left along a short stretch of rough road to join a better road, maintaining your direction.

Soon you fork right uphill as waymarked. Ignore a track to the right and continue ahead. You continue to a summit where the track forks: take the right fork to carry on more steeply uphill as directed by the waymark post. *A little seat on the left provides the opportunity for some respite before you continue this quite substantial climb.* You pass the farm of Bryn Cownwy down to the left, which provides visual interest in this quite enclosed valley. At the top of the climb you cross a forest track and carry on ahead as waymarked up a thankfully less steep incline. Stay on the track as it swings left and then goes downhill as waymarked.

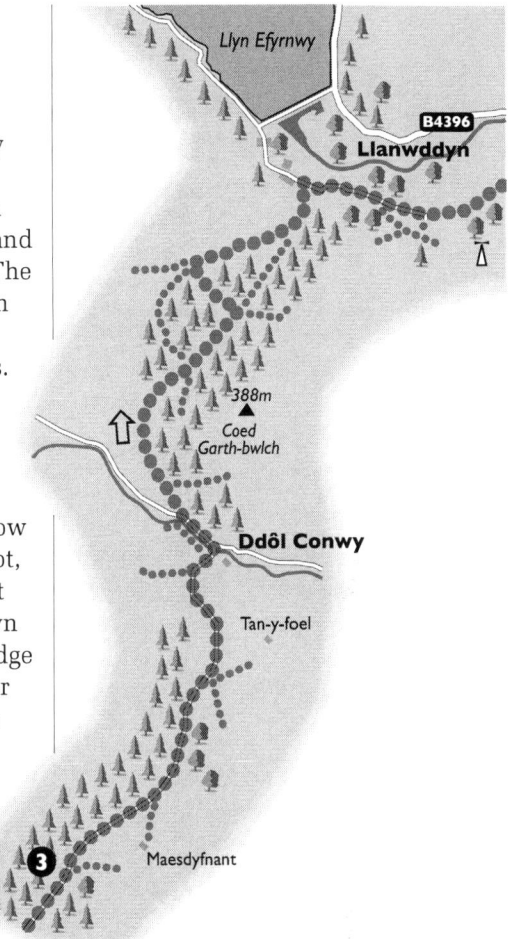

71

The dam at Llanwddyn

Eventually you pass a waymark post to emerge at a track junction. Cross straight over the junction and then immediately turn right to climb a stile by a gate, with the dam at Lake Vyrnwy in view ahead. Now walk downhill with the fence to your right. Pass a waymark post and carry on downhill – *enjoying fine views over the lake. The small green building you can see is a weather station.* A boardwalk takes you over a marshy patch to a stile, which you cross and veer right, to walk with the fence to your right. Climb a stile beside a gate and carry on ahead along a track which joins from the right. *There is now an excellent view of the dam, with Pont Cynon beyond and the massive extent of the reservoir hidden away to the left.* You descend behind houses to a road and a red telephone box to turn left, passing the old post office. Ignore a path down to the right and continue ahead to the RSPB centre, café, cycle hire and the audio-visual Lake Vyrnwy Experience.

14 • LLANWDDYN to DOLANOG

8¼ miles

Cycles can be hired from the café at Llanwddyn, and it is a level 12-mile ride around Lake Vyrnwy if you fancy a break from walking! The RSPB has an excellent shop, and a bird hide. The Lake Vyrnwy 3-D Experience, which opened in 2001, can take you on an exciting virtual tour of the lake, and a separate video will give you an insight into the 24,000 acre Lake Vyrnwy Estate's sustainability and biodiversity. Grazing is restricted in the area to promote re-growth, and there are around 90 species of bird regularly breeding here. The Lake Vyrnwy Hotel, just north-east of the dam, is thankfully open to non-residents. With SSSIs, nature trails, a sculpture trail and excellent fishing for brown trout, it is an area worth far more than a fleeting visit.

1 Having visited Lake Vyrnwy you retrace your steps to the village, passing the old post office on your right and the telephone box on your left to walk along a minor road as waymarked, passing the Coedwig Dderw sessile oak forest. You climb gently to reach a fork in the road, where you go left as waymarked towards Grwn Oer. As the lane climbs gently and swings to the left you go to the right, going through a gate at Grwn Oer. Continue past the barn and go through a gate on the right, ignoring the gate ahead, to pass the house up to your right. By the house go through a gate by the house and continue, walking along a green lane at the edge of woodland. Pass through the next gate and carry on along the path by the side of the wood, where you might well find yourself completely surrounded by pheasants! *Some are inquisitive and come quite close, others panic and flap away through the fence, causing quite a commotion.* Leave the fenced track through a gate and turn left to walk downhill along a farm track. Cross a bridge over the Afon Efyrnwy, pass through a metal gate ahead, walk up to the road and turn right.

Now walk along the broad grass verge, climbing gently and eventually ignoring a track to the right to continue ahead as waymarked. Gradually the view to your right opens, providing a welcome distraction from the traffic on the road. Ignore a minor road which forks to the right and maintain your direction towards a waymark post by a wooden bus shelter.

2 Leave the main road and carry on ahead along a minor road to reach a large Forestry Commission sign for Dyfnant Forest, where you fork left through a wooden gate. You now walk along a forest road which climbs gently, still with fine views to the right. Continue ahead as waymarked when a track leaves to the left, and continue to

73

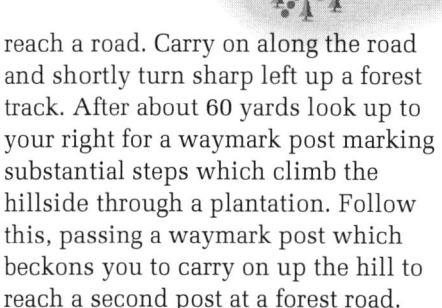

reach a road. Carry on along the road and shortly turn sharp left up a forest track. After about 60 yards look up to your right for a waymark post marking substantial steps which climb the hillside through a plantation. Follow this, passing a waymark post which beckons you to carry on up the hill to reach a second post at a forest road.

Turn left here. Continue to eventually step around a metal barrier to join a forest road and turn right. A waymark post encourages you to carry on, soon enjoying fine views to the left. When the track bends to the left, look out for a waymark post to the right, which directs you to leave the main track and enter the forest to the right. Continue along this path, which can become quite overgrown with bracken during late summer, soon to reach a stile in a fence by a tumbled stone wall. Cross this and continue slightly right as directed. Cross the brow of the hill and head towards a stile in the fence to your right. *The view here is splendid.* Cross the stile to enter an area of forest and veer left. Descend along a vague path through woodland to head towards a stile in the fence at the bottom of the slope. Cross this stile and turn right. Walk with the fence to your right until

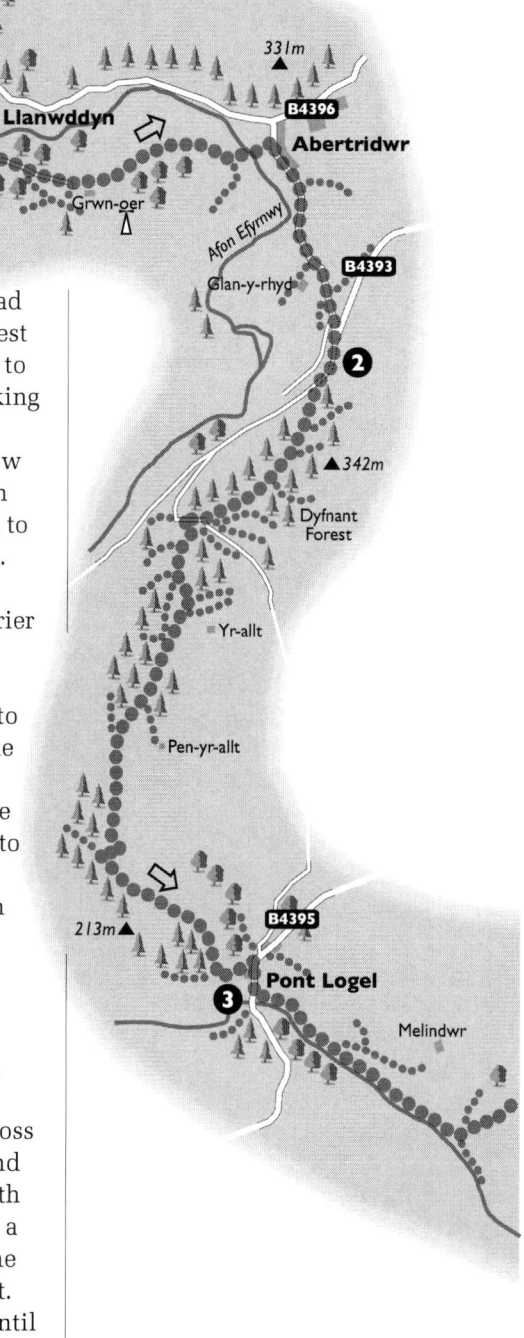

14 • Llanwddyn to Dolanog

you reach steps. Go down them and turn left to walk with the fence on the right. When you reach a stile beside a gate on the right, cross it and walk down the track. After about 100 yards you join a track and turn sharp left. Soon this track peters out and you veer left up a path to a waymark post by a gap in a stone wall. Go through the gap and carry on ahead along a track under mature trees to reach a gate. Go through this and carry on along the hillside, gradually descending and eventually joining a fence to your left. When you reach a gate and a stile, cross the stile and carry on with a stone wall and woods to your right. Having passed by the remains of some very ancient farm machinery you go through a gate to enter a caravan park. Turn sharp left and walk towards a church. Walk to the left of this, by the green corrugated iron Llwydiarth village hall to descend to the road, where you pass through a gate and turn right.

3 At Pont Llogel, where the bridge was built in 1818, there is a prettily situated church standing almost at the edge of Parc Newydd, at one time a medieval deer park enclosing 1000 acres, and owned by the Fychan family. Sir Gruffudd Fychan was an ally of Owain Glyndŵr during the uprising. This is the start of The Pererindod Melangell Walk, a 15-mile linear route between the Vyrnwy and Tanat Valleys which was once used by drovers, quarrymen and pilgrims, who visited the church of St Melangell, all that survives of a nunnery built some 1400 years ago. There is a post office and garage here, both looking very dapper.

Carry on along Glyndŵr's Way, walking below the church at Pont Llogel to reach the Forestry Commission sign for Pont Llogel on your left. Here you turn left just before the bridge, as waymarked, to enter the forest. You now walk along an excellent path beside the Afon Vyrnwy – through a SSSI rich with oak and hazel, and sharing the route with the Ann Griffiths Bible Walk. Ignore forest walks which are signposted to the left and continue ahead, with the river tumbling over falls through deciduous trees to the right. You pass low rocky cliffs on your left and eventually reach a gate by the Vyrnwy. Cross this and carry on with the river on your right, to reach a gated wooden bridge. Cross this and, saying goodbye to the Ann Griffiths Walk,

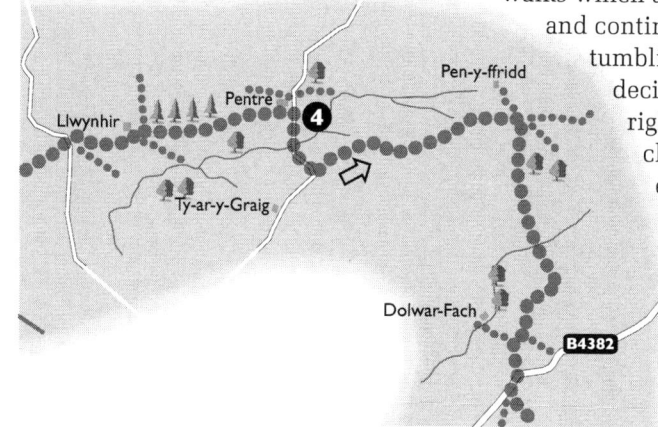

75

Keep walking as directed

you continue ahead up the bwlch with trees and the stony bed of a stream to your right.

Keeping the fence to your right you reach the top of the hill. Pass a gate on your right and continue beside a fence and a ditch to a second gate on the right. Go through this and turn left. Climb to a stile in the field corner, cross it and carry on ahead, keeping the ditch to your left. When you reach a gate, go through and cross the road and carry on ahead, through a gate as waymarked, towards Llwyn Hir farm. You walk along the driveway to the farm, then pass through gates into the farmyard and veer left to cross the yard and leave through a gate, turning right to walk behind the barn to a gate. Go through and, ignoring the gate immediately ahead, walk up the track to the left of it, keeping the fence to your right. This very pleasant green track now gently winds its way uphill with fine views over rolling green countryside to the right. Continue ahead.

When you reach a small wooden gate, go through and carry on ahead to a small wooden gate above a farm building. Go through this and carry on ahead. Pass through a metal gate and turn right, walk through two more metal gates and then veer left to join a road at Pentre farm.

4 Turn right along this road and follow it downhill as it descends into a dingle and then climbs, passing a small quarry on the left. When you reach the top of the hill, and the road swings to the right, you turn left along a track as waymarked, resuming your gentle climb. When the track reaches its summit, ignore a gate to the right and carry on ahead to a gate. Go through and continue ahead. Walk along a wide open track to reach a stile beside a gate. Cross the stile and now walk along a much more enclosed track with trees and bushes either side – you will need to pick your way around some muddy sections. A waymark post reassures you that

14 • Llanwddyn to Dolanog

you are following the correct route through bracken and the low branches of the hedge.

As you walk along this track keep a close look out for a stile beside a gate on the right (easily missed), below the low summit of Fridd Llwydiarth to the north. Cross this stile and walk with the old fence and hedge to your left. Pass through an old metal gate and continue ahead, crossing a tiny stream. Walk up to a waymark post and continue ahead as directed, with the fence on your right. Ignore a metal gateway to your right, and continue ahead, ignoring a second gate on the right and continuing down to a stile, which you cross and carry on ahead, keeping the fence to your right. *There is now a fine view over the Vyrnwy valley.* Carry on to a stile, cross this and turn sharp right to walk with a hedge and a fence to your right. The path descends the field to a stile on the right – cross this and carry on with the fence now to the left. Walk to a waymark post at the edge of a steep slope and turn right to carry on down to a stile at Dolwar Fach.

Cross the stile, clamber down to the lane, and turn left. Leave Dolwar Fach through impressive white gateposts with sturdy metal gates, join a road and turn right. Walk along the road for about 30 yards, and then veer off left to cross a stile and walk ahead over a rough and scrubby field, where sheep attempt to eat what is left of the grass, following waymark posts over the common. *The view behind you is quite pleasant, with rolling hills separated by wooded valleys.* Eventually you join an old track and continue up the hill as directed by a waymark post, once again sharing the route with the Ann Griffiths Walk. You are now gently climbing the side of Allt Dolanog, which is topped by the banks and ditches of a hill fort. As you continue up the rough hillside, following the waymarks and crossing a boardwalk to eventually emerge from the bracken to join a track. Continue ahead as waymarked. Go through a metal gate to join a rough tarmac road and continue ahead along this extremely attractive valley. You pass the chapel and descend to Dolanog (the dale of the salmon) – *the childhood home of Ann Griffiths (1776-1805), the 18th century Calvinistic Methodist hymn writer, who died in childbirth following her marriage to Thomas Griffiths of Meifod. She lived in Dolwar Fach.* Turn left by what was the post office, which before that was the village blacksmith's.

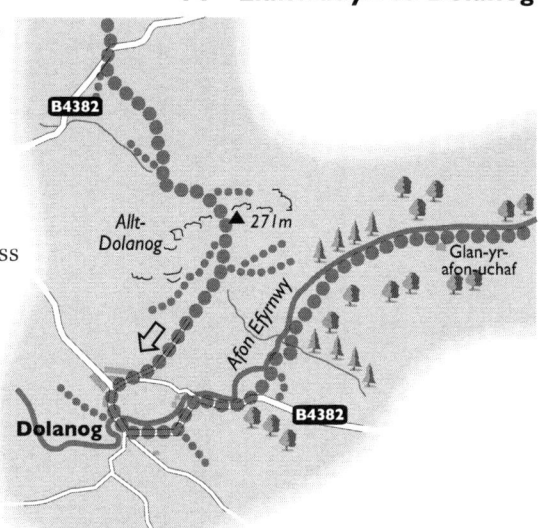

77

Glyndŵr's Way

15 • DOLANOG to MEIFOD

10¾ miles

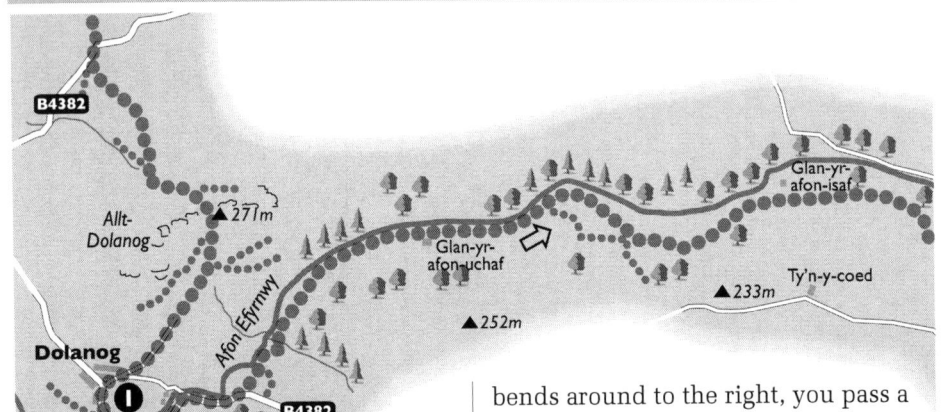

From Dolanog walk along the main road, passing the church on your right, continuing across the old bridge and ignoring a road which joins from the right. *Down to your left, glimpsed through trees, the Afon Efyrnwy tumbles over stones and shallow falls to reach a quite dramatic weir, where the water falls over a sheer drop marking the upstream limit for salmon, who put on a display each autumn when they try, unsuccessfuly, to leap this obstacle. Water from these falls once powered a turbine which supplied electricity for the village. The river here is now noted mainly for brown trout, and fish of up to 4 lbs have been caught.* Carry on along the main road as waymarked, still with the river to your left. When the road bends around to the right, you pass a metal field gate and walk up to a stile on the left. Cross this and turn right to walk across a field to a second stile. Climb this and continue ahead as waymarked, with the river still to your left. You now follow what is intitially a fine rocky path along the top of a steep defile, passing through dense mixed woodland. You cross a small bridge and a gate, turn left and continue.

When the path temporarily leaves the river-side, follow the waymark posts, crossing a stile and following the path through more old mixed woodland and bracken. Climb a stile through an old overgrown hedge and carry on, soon passing Glan-yr-afon-uchaf to your right, a pretty little rickety cottage. A waymark post confirms you are still on the correct route.

Shortly after a fence joins your route on the right you go through a gate and finally part company with

15 • Dolanog to Meifod

the river to continue ahead along a rough track and then uphill, passing a small conifer plantation on the left and heading towards Gwern-fawr. When you reach the house veer left along the path (do not enter the grounds) and go through a gate to your right, then turn left to walk along the lane.

the village has supported two iron forges, three grain mills and a woollen factory, along with two grocer's shops, a haberdasher, a cobbler and a blacksmith. Hendafarn, near the bridge, used to be a drover's inn.

The John Hughes Memorial Chapel (Hen Capel John Hughes) and cottage, built in Pontrobert in 1800, was the home for 40 years of the weaver who went on to keep a day school, joined the Calvinistic Methodists and started preaching in 1800. Eventually he became a full-time minister at Bala in 1814. His wife, Ruth, was formerly

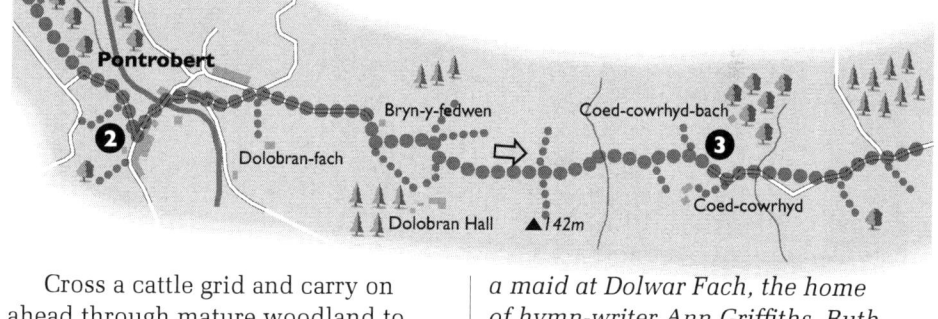

Cross a cattle grid and carry on ahead through mature woodland to cross a second cattle grid and continue along the clear route, a very pleasant change from the usual intricacies of Glyndŵr's Way. The prominent and distinctive cone-like summit of Bryngwyn appears to the left above the more typical gentle wooded hills of the valley. When a track joins from the left continue ahead to join a minor road and turn left as signposted.

2 Soon you turn left to follow the main road at Pontrobert – *a village of mainly new, and a few not so new, houses, which takes its name from Oliver ap Robert, who built the first bridge here in 1670. Over the centuries*

a maid at Dolwar Fach, the home of hymn-writer Ann Griffiths. Ruth read the poems which Ann Griffiths had recited to her – John transcribed them and they were published by the Rev Thomas Charles in 1806. Each year August 12th is celebrated as Ann Griffiths Day. The fully restored building was re-opened in 1995, and there is a programme of day retreats (ring Nia Rhosier on 01938 500631 for details). The chapel is open 14.00–18.00 Tue–Fri, and Sat & Sun by arrangement. Closed Mon. There is no charge, but donations are welcomed.

Cross the bridge, with the church over to your left, and then turn right as signposted towards Meifod. At the next road junction veer left as

79

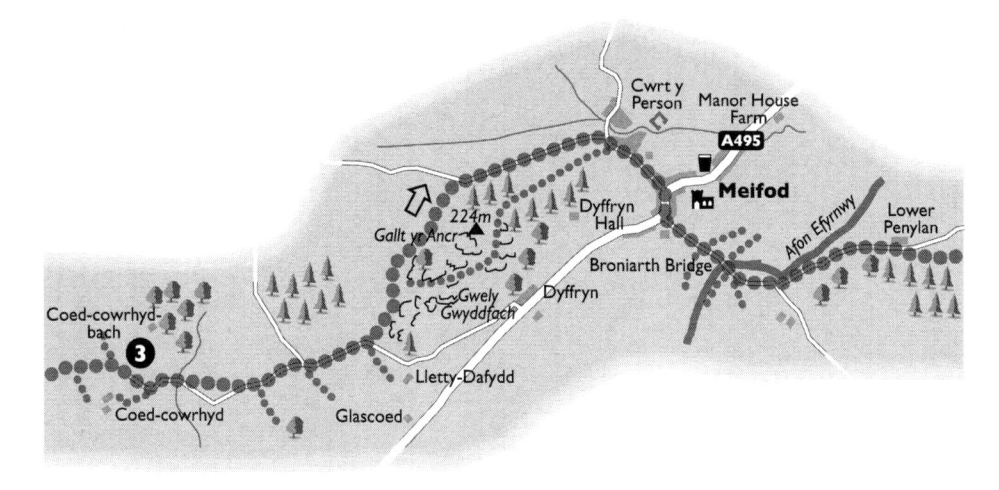

signposted to pass the Royal Oak pub on the left. *Here you can get a meal all day, children are welcome, and there is accommodation.* When you reach a crossroads by a pretty little red and cream brick chapel 'Sion' turn right along the ungated road, ignoring a gated track to the right. You pass the entrance to Bryn-y-fedwen and veer right, staying on the track, as waymarked. Go through a gate beside a gate and then walk to the left downhill along a track with a hedge to your left and a pleasant view to your right. At the bottom of the track go through a gate and turn right, ignoring the gates ahead and to your left. Climb a short hill, turn left through a gate and then turn right to walk with the hedge to your right. At the field corner ignore the gate ahead and turn left to walk up the field with the fence and a conifer plantation to your right.

You are now on the brow of a hill, with a view of a gentle valley to your left and trees to your right. Soon you pass a waymark post, and continue ahead as directed. When you reach a gate in the field corner, go through it and continue ahead, with views over the Vyrnwy valley now opening to your right. Pass through gateless posts and walk downhill, with trees and a house to your right. You reach a waymark post and walk to the right of it to enter an old green lane, which soon swings gently left to a waymark post, where you turn right along a farm track to reach a farm gate over a stream. Go through and continue along a track towards a gate. Don't go through this but continue with the fence to your right. When you reach a pedestrian gate in the hedgeline go through and continue up the meadow as directed by the waymark to reach a stone track on the far side. Turn right here as directed. Pass through a field gate and soon reach a finger post, which directs you along a minor road which winds gently downhill to reach a track entrance on the left.

15 • Dolanog to Meifod

Summer in Meifod

3 Cross the stile which is directly ahead of you here and walk diagonally across the field to reach a stile in the opposite corner, by the scant remains of an old hedge. Cross this stile, descend to the lane and turn left to walk uphill between tall hedges. When you reach a junction continue ahead as directed by a waymark post. Shortly after the lane veers to the right, turn off left, as signposted, through a gate near a field gate to follow a rough track to emerge onto a rocky summit. Continue as directed by the waymark above and past a small enclosure to meet the edge of a wood. Walk down the side of the wood to join a track. A short stretch of track brings you to a gate, which you go through and carry on ahead along a hedged green lane.

Gallt yr Ancr (Anchorite's Hill), to your right, has a pillow mound near the top, known as Gwely Gwyddfarch (Gwyddfarch's bed), and is said to mark the last resting place of the saint who founded the church in Meifod around 550 AD. Parts of this basic oak-framed building are thought to have survived until the 17th century, when they were covered by Church Walk. The track then descends beside a thick forest plantation. Go through a field gate to reach a road continue ahead and then, at a T junction, turn right to walk down to the centre of Meifod passing the handsome new village hall on the left. You meet the main road opposite the old post office. Turn right to continue the walk. The King's Head, serving meals and real ale, is along the road to the left.

… Glyndŵr's Way

16 • MEIFOD to WELSHPOOL

7 miles

1 Walk past what was once the Post Office in Meifod, on the left, and then turn left at the road signposted towards Guilsfield, passing a beautifully converted chapel on the right, followed by tennis courts and a bowling green on the left. Cross Broniarth Bridge over the Afon Vyrnwy, in the midst of a wide valley. Stay on the road as it bends gently left, with the buildings of Pen-y-lan Hall ahead: the old stables looking far more charming than the house from this viewpoint. At the next junction turn left to walk along Ffordd Glyndŵr, which climbs gently, with the river down to the left. As you pass the entrance to Pen lan Isaf look for the track which leaves to the right, and follow this steeply up into attractive mixed woodland. When the main forest track hairpins to the right you continue ahead as waymarked. Soon woods become a forest plantation, with regular rows of conifers, as the track continues steeply up Broniarth Hill.

Again when the forest track swings sharply right, you carry on ahead along a path as waymarked, continuing your climb – *with excellent views over the Vyrnwy valley opening to your left.* Pass through a wooden gate and carry on ahead, once again walking through mixed deciduous woodland. Go through a gate above a little red-brick hut within an enclosure, and continue ahead, leaving the woodland behind.

Now immediately turn left as directed by the waymark and carry on walking with a fence to your right. *Down to your right is Llyn Du.* Ignore a gateway on your right and continue up the hill by the electricity poles, as waymarked. When you reach the end of the hedge on the right, turn sharply right to walk down to a gate, which you then go through to join a lane, where you turn right.

2 You now follow a lane which gives occasional glimpses of the lake down to your right. Continue straight ahead at a crossroads as waymarked. Carry on ahead when a track joins from the left, still climbing gently. At the top of the incline a very fine view over the Banwy valley opens to the right and eventually you reach a road junction, where you fork right and walk gently downhill.

As the road begins to descend more steeply and swings away to the right you turn sharp left to cross a stile beside an old gate, to walk along an overgrown track. Cross a second stile beside a gate and continue ahead as directed by a waymark post: you are now walking across a grassy hill-slope towards trees. Carry on as directed by the next waymark post through a gap in the trees to follow the vestiges of a track towards a gate ahead, overlooked by a corrugated iron barn standing next to the diminutive ruin of Ty Newydd.

16 • Meifod to Welshpool

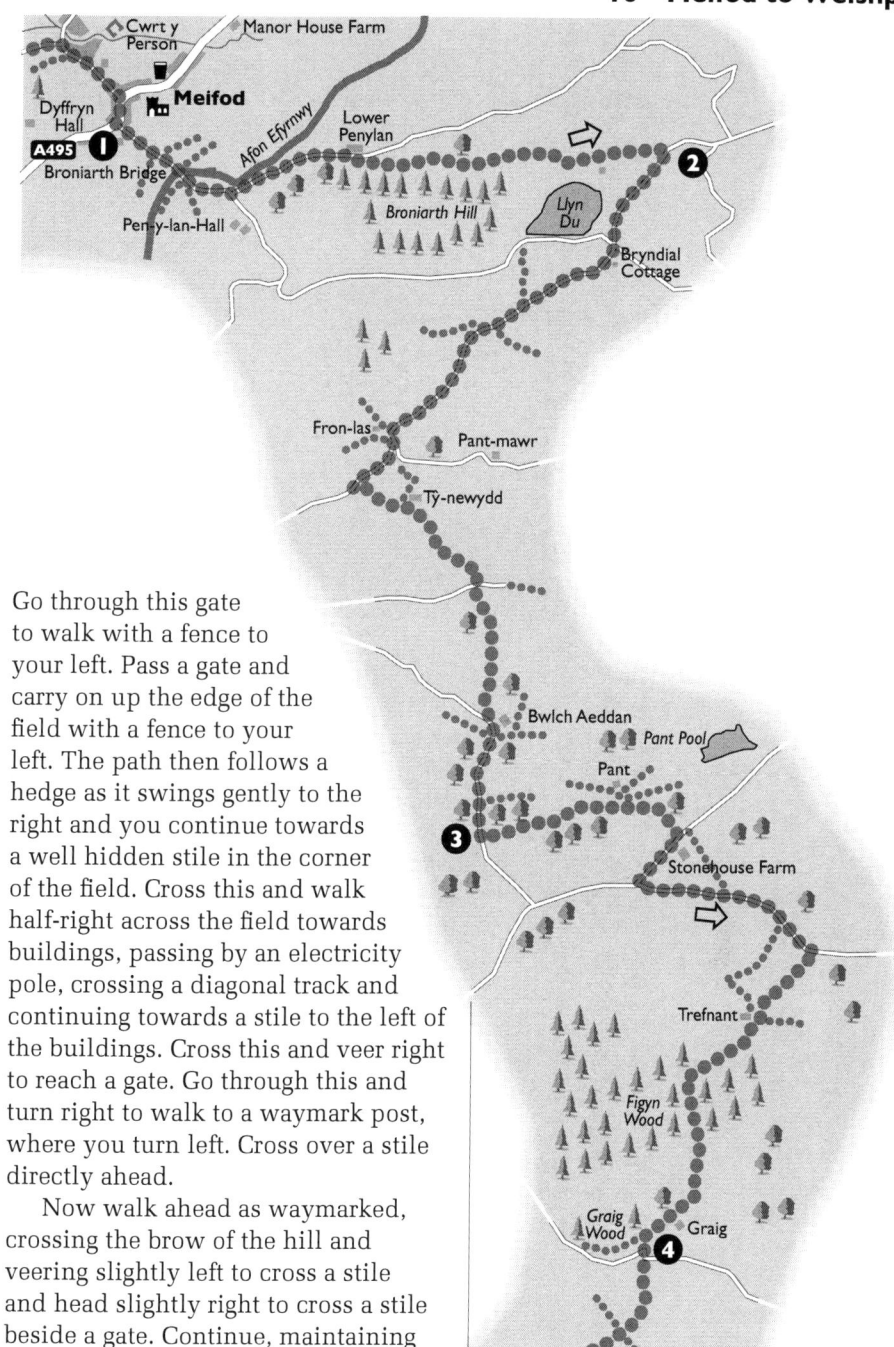

Go through this gate to walk with a fence to your left. Pass a gate and carry on up the edge of the field with a fence to your left. The path then follows a hedge as it swings gently to the right and you continue towards a well hidden stile in the corner of the field. Cross this and walk half-right across the field towards buildings, passing by an electricity pole, crossing a diagonal track and continuing towards a stile to the left of the buildings. Cross this and veer right to reach a gate. Go through this and turn right to walk to a waymark post, where you turn left. Cross over a stile directly ahead.

Now walk ahead as waymarked, crossing the brow of the hill and veering slightly left to cross a stile and head slightly right to cross a stile beside a gate. Continue, maintaining your direction and climbing gently up

83

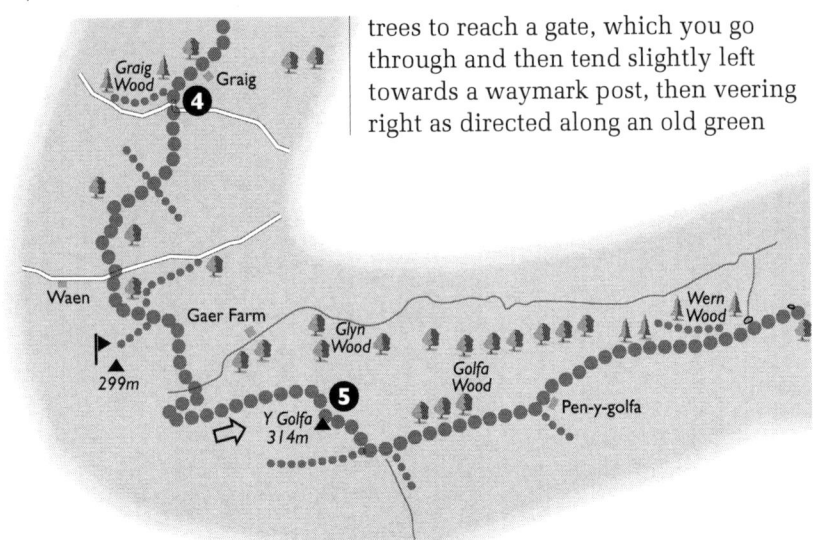

towards woods, where a waymark post can be seen.

When you reach the perimeter of the woodland turn right to walk with the fence and the trees to your left, enjoying open views on your right towards Gwely Gwyddfarch, by Meifod. Soon you descend to cross a stile to the right of a gate. Cross this to step down to a road and turn left, following the road as in swings around to the right.

Ignore the entrance to Bwlch Aeddan on your left and carry on up the hill. A waymark reassures you as you pass Pant Pool in the distance to your left. *To your right is the Big Forest – a name that flatters.* When the road begins to swing to the left, look out for a finger post which directs you to go through a small metal gate on the left to enter Kennel Wood.

3 Follow the rough path, with a dingle to your left, ignoring a wooden gate to the right, through the trees to reach a gate, which you go through and then tend slightly left towards a waymark post, then veering right as directed along an old green trackway below a red-brick house. The track climbs and then turns left by a fence, ignoring a metal gate ahead. Continue with the fence to your right, overlooking a valley to your left. When the fence swings away to your right, you continue ahead along a track, as waymarked. Carry on along a clear track, pass through a metal gate and walk ahead, ignoring tracks which leave your route on the left and right. Go through a wooden gate and veer right to walk up the lane, passing pretty landscaped pools and the gardens of a caravan park down to your left. *On a hot sunny day the swimming pool here could look very enticing!* Follow the lane as it swings to the right, passing the Hidden Valley Chalet Park and continuing up the hill to reach a road, opposite Stonehouse Farm, where you turn right.

Carefully walk along the road, using the verge to avoid traffic, and as you reach the top of the hill, where the main road swings around to the right,

16 • Meifod to Welshpool

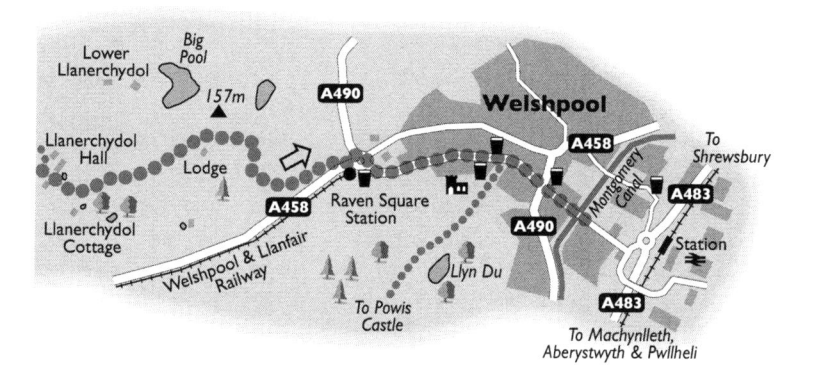

turn sharply left by a post box, passing a handsome old red-brick school building, converted to a residence and a B&B. Pass a disused quarry on the right and continue. Waymark posts reassure you as you walk along the lane until it gently descends and swings to the left: here you look out for a stile on the right. Cross it and walk to the right as directed by the waymark post. Gradually you part company with the fence on your right to reach a waymark post ahead. Pass through a gap in the trees and carry on diagonally down the field towards a large tree, with the fence over to your right. Walk through a line of trees, then swing left down to a waymark post in front of corrugated iron buildings. When you reach the double concrete farm track follow it for about 10 yards, and then swing around to the left to go through the gate ahead of you. Walk down the field with the fence to your right, and then turn right through a gate at the bottom.

Now walk ahead and, when two gates appear in front of you, don't go through them but turn left to cross over a ditch and a gate beside a field gate, then turn right to walk with the ditch to your right. When you reach a gate, go through it and carry on ahead along a rough path through re-growing woodland. When you reach a waymark post in Figyn Wood, turn sharp left. Climb up the steep track through the trees, cross a forest road and continue ahead following a scant line of deciduous trees, stopping now and again to catch your breath and enjoy the view. Leave the wood through a gate and veer half-right, ignoring a gate to your left to walk towards a stile, which you cross and carry on ahead. Ignore waymarks which direct you to the right and, when you reach a gate, go through and continue down the green track until a waymark post directs you to branch off to the right, by trees, along a very rough path. Continue ahead into Woodland Trust

85

land. *This is Graig Wood, an 8-acre wood dominated by sessile oak, with ash, beech, sycamore, crab apple, rowan and field maple. There is hazel, holly, hawthorn and blackthorn in the shrub layer, with bluebells, wood sage, wood anenome, violet, red campion, honeysuckle and primrose at ground level. The woodland is being allowed to naturally regenerate.*

4 When you reach a gate go through it and, after about 25 yards, turn left as directed by a waymark post to descend steps to a road. Turn right to soon turn left off the road through a field gate by a finger post. Walk downhill towards a stile a little to the right of the field corner. Cross this and turn left, following the fence line to a waymark post in the corner. Walk down towards a copse, keeping it to your right. Pass alongside the copse, looking for a gate over a ditch. Go through and follow the fence line on the right (ignoring gates in the fence) to a stile. Cross this and go down steps to a minor road. Cross the road, cross a stile and turn half-right to walk over a field. Keep a quarried area to your left, following a track around it to reach a stile. Cross this onto Golfa. Now look for the waymark post which directs you through woods and gorse to emerge by a 'tee' on the golf course. Walk around this as directed to reach a path with a handrail. Climb to a waymark post, then continue to descend to a waymark post, which beckons you to veer left, following the line of the fence and crossing a very rough and very wet hollow on a boardwalk to a waymark post just showing above the bracken on the far side. When you reach this post, turn sharp right to walk towards the next waymark post. Continue uphill, climbing and veering to the left. You eventually emerge from the bracken and swing left to walk along the top of the hillside. *The view from here is magnificent, in a sweep from the north-west to the north-east.* Continue along the edge of the golf course, following the waymark posts as they appear, but noting the direction indicated as soon you have to turn sharply right to climb steeply up the summit of Y Golfa: 1119 ft high and topped by an Ordnance Survey trig. point. *Now the view is equally stupendous, but this time encompassing the whole 360 degree panorama.*

5 Leave the summit as directed by the waymark post and follow the clear green path downhill. When the path splits, go to the right as directed and then veer left downhill, following the posts and entering bracken. Eventually you reach a gate, which you go through and carry on ahead, with a fence and trees to your left. Cross a stile beside a metal gate and continue ahead. *Across the valley to your right is the track of the Welshpool & Llanfair Steam Railway, which opened in 1903, and in the summer you may be lucky enough to see a steam train journeying between Llanfair Caereinion and Welshpool.* Go through a gate and carry on ahead, veering slightly left to walk with a broken hedgerow to your right and picking-up a track which swings left and then right to walk with a forest plantation on your left. Go through

16 • Meifod to Welshpool

Only a few yards to go now – fancy a pint?

a gate and carry on along the track. *To the left, beyond Wern Wood, is an attractive and very productive area of nursery gardens.* Go through a gate and continue ahead with the fence now to the right.

Pass the pond at Llanerchydol Home Farm and walk down to a gate. Go through and carry on descending, passing another pond. Cross a cattle grid by a gate and follow a wide track through parkland by Llanerchydol Hall, eventually joining a tarmac road. Stay on the road as it continues through mixed woodland, passing some magnificently large and gnarled old oak trees – and a well-restored gate-house.

As your descent continues the sound of traffic announces the approach of Welshpool, and soon you are enjoying a fine view over this busy border town. Cross a cattle grid opposite Raven Square Station and fork left to descend to a road, where you turn right. At Raven Square roundabout carefully cross to walk up the road signed to the Town Centre, passing the Raven Inn *(food available most days)* on your right. Cross the road to walk along the pavement as Raven Street becomes Mount Street. Pass some very enticing pubs as you continue ahead – *perhaps taking a look at the restored octagonal cockpit just to the right, off the main street. It is thought to be the only one in Wales which survives on its original site.* You reach traffic lights by the Royal Oak Hotel. Carry on ahead to reach the Powisland Museum and Montgomery Canal Centre – *a traditional wharf and warehouse c.1880, now housing a museum illustrating the archaeology, history and literature of the local area. It includes a canal exhibition and a display featuring the Montgomeryshire Yeomanry Cavalry.* You have reached the end of Glyndŵr's Way! There is also a small canalside garden over

87

Glyndŵr's Way

The canal basin, Welshpool. You've made it!

the bridge on the left where you can loosen your laces and put your feet up for a while.

Welshpool was described in 1822 as being 'a large and populous town, and the appearance of opulence is very predominant throughout the place, perhaps owing to its trade in Welsh flannels, which is carried on here to a very great extent. The corner stones whereon its prosperity is founded are the flannel trade and the canal'. Originally the streets were lined with smart town houses, backed with gardens, but this ground was soon needed to build housing for workers in the tanning and flannel industries who lived, along with their pigs and their cess pits, in appalling squalor in what were known as 'shuts'. In 1848 there was a cholera epidemic which originated from the Lledan Brook and the Llyndu Stream, giving the town at that time the highest mortality rate in North Wales.

St Mary's church is just up the road from the Royal Oak, and nearby is Grace Evans' Cottage. Grace was the maid of Lady Nithsdale, a daughter of the Earl of Powis whose husband, a Jacobite leader, was being held in the Tower of London in 1715, awaiting execution. Grace helped Lady Nithsdale rescue her husband, and was given the cottage in recognition of this bravery. A glacial boulder near the south porch of the church is said to have been used by Druids.

By the early 20th century Welshpool had become predominantly a market town, its earlier manufacturing prosperity having faded. Today it is a base for light industry, and during the summer many visitors come to visit Powis Castle about a mile outside the town – a restored medieval castle which has been continuously inhabited for over 500 years. On display are fine paintings, tapestries, early Georgian furniture and relics of Clive of India. The 18th century terraced gardens are superb.

The Montgomeryshire Canal

Glyndŵr's Way reaches its official end in an inauspicious garden beside the canal bridge in Welshpool. But just the other side of the bridge is Welshpool Lock and the Powysland Museum – and both are a far more interesting and fitting end to your walk!

The opening of the Montgomeryshire Canal in 1796 contributed greatly to the town's prosperity, and eventually the Shropshire Union Canal Company made Welshpool the administrative centre for their Welsh region, and an extensive group of buildings were erected around the wharf in Severn Street, enclosed by a sandstone wall, perhaps to keep this industry away from the eyes of the Earls of Powis. A terrace of these buildings are still standing and, if you peep through the window of the house closest to the road, you can see the clerk still keeping his ledger up to date. The cottage next door was originally a salt warehouse, later to become the lock-keeper's cottage. Number 3 was a joiners shop, 4 was the residence of the owner of a local corn-mill, and 5 was a house and warehouse.

The Powisland Museum occupies what was once a granary/warehouse. It was founded by the Powysland Club in 1874, and was transferred under trust to the town of Welshpool to mark the Jubilee of Queen Victoria in 1887. It moved to this building in 1990. The displays illustrate the history and development of life in Montgomeryshire from the earliest prehistoric settlers to the 20th century population. On show are exhibits reflecting the history of local agriculture and crafts, the Victorian kitchen, the canal and railway systems, the Montgomeryshire Yeomanry Cavalry and World War I. A wonderful collection of old maps and photographs is also on show. *It is open Mon, Tue, Thur-Sat 11.00-13.00 & 14.00-17.00 (Oct-Apr Sat 14.00-17.00). Modest admission charge.* The old canal-maintenance yard is now occupied by a builder's merchants – it once contained a small internal railway system.

When the main line railway came to Welshpool trade on the waterway dwindled, and it closed in 1944 following a disastrous breach in 1936 at the Perry Aqueduct, near Frankton. Since the 1960s there has been an energetic campaign for eventual complete restoration, and this now seems assured, although progress is slow.

Guidance Notes & Useful Information

Preparing for your walk

Preparation is important so, if you have never tried hill walking, test yourself over a few days or weekends before deciding to take on Glyndŵr's Way. Many young people find they are naturally fit but lack stamina; older people still have the potential for excellent stamina but lack basic strength. It is never too late to get fit, but the older you are, the more gentle should be the programme. Some kind of exercise which makes you sweaty and breathless for 20 minutes every two or three days is an ideal level of preparation, to be built up gradually. If you can cope with this, a day or two on Glyndŵr's Way should hold no fears at all. However, to cope with the whole walk, day after day, requires extra stamina which can only be earned the hard way – on the hills.

To avoid blisters or sore feet, boots should be waterproof and thoroughly worn in, and socks should be absorbent, without lumpy seams. Hardening the skin on the soles and heels helps, and this can be assisted by applying alcohol or surgical spirit for a few weeks before a big walk. If blisters form, prick them and apply a porous plaster to keep the dead skin in place over the tender new layer underneath. Keep your toe nails clipped and make sure your boots fit properly.

Your first-aid kit should contain plasters, pain-relief tablets, something to treat diarrhoea, something to treat midge bites and insect repellent. Lip salve can help wind-dried lips and Vaseline can help to soothe sore or chapped skin. It is best to know a little about first aid, and to be aware of the treatment for gastroenteritis (drink clear fluids with glucose and a little salt) and exposure (glucose, warm dry clothing and a quick walk to shelter).

Essential clothing for a day on Glyndŵr's Way should include a set of waterproofs (cagoule, overtrousers), a pair of warm trousers and a pullover. You may not need any of these items, but they should be packed in your rucksack just in case. There is no need to invest in heavyweight mountain boots. Lighter walking boots with ankle support, to reduce the risk of sprained ankles, and a degree of waterproofing, are quite adequate. Fully enclosed gaiters (such as the Yeti type) will help keep your lower legs and feet dry even after a wet day above Dylife. A good waterproof rucksack is essential. Into this should go a compass, a Swiss Army Knife or folding multi-

Guidance Notes & Useful Information

tool, a couple of pencils, a set of appropriate maps, and of course don't forget this book!

Food and an adequate supply of drink (clean, fresh, plain water is probably best) and money complete the basic list, to which can be added a camera, mobile phone (coverage is patchy) and charger, sunglasses (we live in hope!), notebook and whatever else you feel inclined to take with you. Company, or the deliberate avoidance of it, will of course be the nub of one of the most important decisions before the start of the walk. Safety, and making sure someone knows where you are, is even more important for lone walkers than it is for groups. Anyone undertaking the whole walk will also need to think carefully about accommodation, for this will affect how much they carry and where they need to pick up provisions.

Planning and accommodation

The tranquil and remote nature of Glyndŵr's Way makes for wonderful walking, but it can present problems with accommodation and baggage. The best way to get up-to-date information is to use the website, which will be found at: www.nationaltrail.co.uk/glyndwrs-way
You will also be able to obtain the latest news of any diversions to the route.

Maps

Glyndŵr's Way is very well waymarked, so setting off with just this book to guide you should be fine. But if you like to adopt a 'belt and braces' approach, the following 1: 25000 scale Ordnance Survey Explorer maps also cover the route: 200, 201, 214, 215, 216 & 239.

The Countryside Code
Be safe - plan ahead and follow any signs
Leave gates and property as you find them
Protect plants and animals, and take your litter home
Keep dogs under close control
Consider other people
Please respect any ancient site visited.

Glyndŵr's Way
Distance checklist

This will assist with planning your walk.

Location   *Approx distance from*
                     previous location

	Miles
Knighton	0
Cefn-suran	5½
Llangunllo	6½
Felindre	9¼
Llanbadarn Fynydd	7½
Abbeycwmhir	8¼
Bwlch-y-Sarnau	3¼
Blaentrinant	6¾
Llanidloes	8½
Afon Biga	9
Aberhosan	9¼
Talbontdrain	2¾
Machynlleth	9½
Penegoes	2½
Abercegir	4¾
Cemmaes Road	8¾
Commins Gwalia	2½
Llanbrynmair	6¾
Llangadfan	10¼
Llanwddyn	6½
Pont Llogel	3½
Dolanog	8¼
Pontrobert	3½
Meifod	7
Welshpool	10¾